HOW TO BE LOVED

7 Simple Steps to Embracing Inner Peace, Breaking Negative Cycles, and Cultivating Healing in Relationships

Oliver Thrive

Contents

Introduction

♥

"The journey to love is not about finding the perfect person, but about perfecting our own capacity for love."

Welcome to "How To Be Loved," a book that is not just a guide but a journey – your journey. It is about finding love in its purest form, which surprisingly starts not with another, but within oneself. This book is based on a simple yet profound understanding: to find love, to be loved, we must first understand and love ourselves. It's not about chasing an ideal partner; it's about becoming the best version of ourselves, capable of both giving and receiving love in its healthiest form.

The path I'm inviting you on is not a typical one. It's not filled with clichéd advice or quick fixes. Instead, it's a journey of introspection, healing, and genuine transformation. Through the '7 Simple Steps' method, this book offers a comprehensive approach to personal growth and relationship healing. These steps are simple, not because they require little effort, but because they are clear, straightforward, and proven to be effective.

Personal Story

Let me share with you a story, a personal one, that illustrates the transformative power of self-awareness and love. It was on a quiet, introspective evening, several years ago, that the seeds of this book were sown. My life, at that time, was a far cry from the harmonious and loving existence I had always envisioned. I was ensnared in a tangle of unsatisfying relationships, both romantic and platonic, each one mirroring back to me an image of myself I could hardly recognize. I found myself asking, "Why does love elude me? Why do I keep falling into the same patterns, the same types of relationships that leave me feeling more alone than ever?"

This journey of self-discovery and transformation didn't begin in a therapist's office, nor did it start with a life-altering event. It started with me, in my small apartment, amidst the quiet hours of the night. It began with a simple, yet profound realization: the common denominator in all my relationships was me. This wasn't about blame or self-reproach; it was about acknowledging my role in my own life narrative.

I recall sitting there, a journal in hand, the blank pages seeming to beckon to my thoughts and confessions. I started writing, not with any particular aim, but simply as a means to pour out the jumble of feelings and thoughts that had long been simmering within me. As the words flowed, patterns began to emerge like stars slowly appearing in the night sky, forming constellations I had never noticed before. I saw my tendency to seek validation from others, my fear of being alone, and my habit of molding myself to fit into the expectations of those around me. I realized that in my quest for love, I had lost the most crucial connection of all – the one with myself.

Over the following weeks and months, I dedicated myself to this journey of self-reflection. I turned to books. Not just any books, but those that spoke of personal growth, mindfulness, and the psychology of relationships. I absorbed the wisdom of authors who had walked this path before me, finding comfort and guidance in their words. However, the most profound lessons came not from these texts, but from the quiet introspection that they inspired within me.

I began to practice mindfulness and learned to be present with myself, to really listen to my own thoughts and feelings. I found that in the stillness, I could hear the whispers of my inner voice, a voice that had been drowned out by the noise of my busy, unfulfilled life. This mindfulness practice gradually opened the door to a deeper understanding of myself – my fears, my desires, and, most importantly, my strengths.

One evening, as I sat watching the sunset from my window, a sense of clarity washed over me. I realized that my search for love had always been outward-focused, dependent on others to fill the void within. It dawned on me that the love I sought needed to be cultivated from within, that I had to become a source of love for myself before I could truly share it with someone else. This epiphany was the first step in reshaping my approach to relationships.

From that point on, my journey took a new direction. I started to explore ways to nurture self-love and self-compassion. I practiced self-care, not just in the form of bubble baths and occasional treats, but as a daily commitment to honoring and caring for myself. I learned to set boundaries, to say no when something didn't feel right, and to say yes to things that brought me genuine joy and fulfillment.

As I continued to grow and evolve, my relationships began to transform. I noticed a shift in the people I attracted into my life – they were kinder, more authentic, more aligned with the person I was becoming. I found that as I became more authentic, the relationships I formed became more genuine. The superficial connections fell away, making room for deeper, more meaningful bonds.

This transformation wasn't quick or easy. It required patience, perseverance, and a willingness to confront uncomfortable truths about myself. But with each step I took, I felt a growing sense of empowerment and peace. I was no longer a passive participant in my love life; I was actively shaping it with intention and self-awareness.

It was through this personal evolution that the '7 Simple Steps' were born. Each step represents a significant milestone on my journey – from cultivating self-awareness to practicing daily gratitude – and embodies the lessons I learned along the way. These steps are more than just theoretical concepts; they are practical, actionable, and born from real-life experience.

As you embark on this journey through the pages of "How To Be Loved," know that it is a path I have walked myself. The steps I share are the ones that led me to a place of inner peace, self-love, and fulfilling relationships. They are simple, not because they require no effort, but because they are clear, focused, and grounded in the reality of personal experience.

The 7 Simple Steps

The '7 Simple Steps' method that you are about to explore in this book was born out of this personal journey. It is distilled from years of learning, not just from my own experiences but also from the wisdom of experts in psychology, spirituality, and relationship dynamics. Each step is designed to guide you on a path of self-discovery and healing, ultimately leading you to a place where you can experience fulfilling and loving relationships.

1. **Cultivating Self-Awareness:** Learn to understand and accept yourself fully.

2. **Healing From Within:** Address past traumas and emotional wounds to free yourself from their hold.

3. **Communicating Authentically:** Develop the courage and skill to express your true self.

4. **Fostering Intimacy and Trust:** Build deeper connections based on mutual respect and understanding.

5. **Embracing Shared Growth:** Grow alongside your loved ones, supporting each other's individual journeys.

6. **Letting Go of What No Longer Serves:** Release old patterns and relationships that hinder your growth.

7. **Celebrating Love Every Day:** Nurture and appreciate love in your life, every single day.

As you embark on this journey, I invite you to do so with an open heart and mind. It's an invitation to an immersive experience of self-discovery and relationship enrichment. Each chapter contains not just insights and knowledge, but also practical exercises, real-life examples, and reflective questions to help you internalize and apply what you learn.

Remember, this journey is as unique as you are. There is no one-size-fits-all approach to love and relationships. What you'll find here are tools and principles that you can adapt and use in a way that resonates with your individual circumstances and experiences.

As you turn the pages, you'll find yourself on a path to deeper self-awareness, more meaningful relationships, and, ultimately, the kind of love that you've always desired and deserved. A love that isn't just about finding the right person, but about being the right person—for yourself and for others.

Welcome to "How To Be Loved;" your journey to love, in its truest sense.

Step One —Cultivating Self-Awareness

♥

"Awareness is like the sun. When it shines on things, they are transformed."

As we embark on this first step of our journey, let's delve into the essence of self-awareness. It's often said that awareness is the sunlight of the soul. Just as the sun illuminates the earth, bringing life and clarity, self-awareness illuminates our inner world, transforming our understanding of ourselves and how we relate to others.

Understanding Yourself:

The foundation of any deep and meaningful relationship is not found in the eyes of another, but in the depths of our own understanding of ourselves. Self-awareness is the cornerstone upon which the temple of love is built. It is about knowing your desires, your fears, your strengths, your weaknesses, your triggers, your patterns, and what makes you uniquely you.

But how do we cultivate this self-awareness? It begins with a commitment to self-exploration. This can be a daunting task, for it requires us to look inward with honesty and courage. It asks us to pause, to reflect, and to confront parts of ourselves that we may have long ignored or buried. Yet this process is essential, for it leads us to a place of profound self-understanding and acceptance.

In my own journey, I found that the simple act of keeping a journal was a powerful tool for self-discovery. Writing down my thoughts, feelings, and experiences helped me to connect the dots of my life. It revealed patterns I had been unaware of and helped me understand my reactions to various situations. I encourage you to start a journal as a safe space for self-reflection. Write without censorship, and let your thoughts and feelings flow onto the page. Over time, this practice will illuminate aspects of yourself that were previously hidden in the shadows.

The quest for self-awareness is akin to embarking on the most important journey of our lives, one that takes us into the deepest realms of our being. This journey is about more than just introspection; it's a transformative process that reshapes our understanding of who we are and how we love.

The Essence of Self-Awareness: Self-awareness is the foundation of any deep and meaningful relationship. It's not found in the gaze of another but within the quiet depths of our own soul. It focuses on coming face-to-face with our true selves – our desires, fears, strengths, and weaknesses. It involves understanding our emotional triggers, the patterns that dictate our behaviors, and the unique qualities that make us who we are.

However, cultivating this self-awareness is not a passive process. It is an active endeavor, requiring a commitment to delve into the uncharted territories of our inner world. This journey calls for honesty, courage, and a willingness to face parts of ourselves that we may have conveniently ignored or buried under the debris of daily living.

The Power of Reflection and Introspection: The path to self-awareness begins with reflection and introspection. It consists of taking a pause from the relentless pace of life, to sit with ourselves, to listen to the whispers of our heart and the cries of our soul. This process of looking inward can be daunting, for it often reveals truths we may not be prepared to face. Yet, it is essential for true growth and understanding.

In my journey, the practice of introspection became a beacon of light. I found solace in the quiet moments of reflection, where I could peel back the layers of my persona, layer by layer, revealing the raw and unfiltered truths of my existence. It was in these moments of solitude that I began to understand the intricacies of my being.

Journaling: A Tool for Discovery: One of the most powerful tools in this journey of self-discovery was keeping a journal. I found that the simple act of writing down my thoughts, feelings, and experiences was profoundly therapeutic. It became a sanctuary where I could express myself freely, without the fear of judgment or the need for validation.

Journaling allowed me to unravel the complexities of my emotions and thoughts. It became a mirror reflecting my inner world, helping me to see and understand patterns of behavior and thought that had previously eluded my awareness. I began to notice how certain events triggered specific emotional responses, how my past was influencing my present, and how my perception of myself was shaping my relationships.

As you embark on this journey, I encourage you to embrace journaling as a tool for self-discovery. Allow yourself the freedom to write without censorship. Let your thoughts and feelings flow onto the pages of your journal. This practice will not only provide clarity but also serve as a record of your journey towards self-awareness.

Uncovering Patterns and Triggers: Through journaling and introspection, you will begin to uncover patterns in your thoughts and behaviors. You might notice recurring themes in your reactions to certain situations or people. This awareness is crucial, as it provides insight into how your past experiences are influencing your present actions and choices.

Understanding your emotional triggers is another critical aspect of self-awareness. Triggers are those moments or events that evoke a strong emotional response, often disproportionate to the situation. By identifying these triggers, you can begin to understand the deeper issues that need your attention and healing.

The Role of Mindfulness in Self-Awareness: Mindfulness is another essential element in cultivating self-awareness. It's the practice of being present in the moment, fully engaged with whatever we are doing, without distraction or judgment. Mindfulness teaches us to observe our thoughts and feelings without getting entangled in them. It helps us to recognize our habitual reactions and choose how we respond to life's challenges.

Incorporating mindfulness into your daily routine can be transformative. It could be as simple as spending a few minutes each day in quiet meditation, focusing on your breath, or practicing mindful eating or walking. The key is to be present and attentive to the now, which is the only moment we truly have.

Acceptance:

The Gateway to Inner Peace: As you journey through the process of self-awareness, you will inevitably encounter aspects of yourself that you may not like or feel comfortable with. This is where the power of acceptance becomes crucial. Acceptance is not about resignation or complacency; it involves acknowledging your truths and embracing yourself, warts and all.

Self-acceptance is the gateway to inner peace. It allows us to let go of self-judgment and self-criticism and embrace a more compassionate view of ourselves. It is in this space of acceptance that we find the freedom to grow, to change, and to cultivate a deeper, more authentic love – for ourselves and others.

The Journey Ahead: As you continue on this path, remember that self-awareness is not a destination but a journey – a continuous process of growth, learning, and evolution. It requires patience, persistence, and, most importantly, a gentle kindness towards oneself.

In the following sections of this chapter, we will explore practical ways to reflect on past relationships and embrace the present moment. These practices are designed to deepen your understanding of yourself and pave the way for a future where love, peace, and fulfillment are not just aspirations but realities.

Embarking on this journey of self-awareness is the first step towards transforming your relationships and finding true love. As you delve into the depths of your being, you will discover a wellspring of wisdom and insight that will guide you in creating the loving, fulfilling relationships you desire.

Reflecting on Past Relationships:

One of the most revealing exercises in cultivating self-awareness is reflecting on our past relationships. Our history in love often holds crucial insights into our deepest emotional patterns and how they have shaped our present.

Think back to your past relationships and consider the roles you played. Were you the caretaker, always putting the needs of your partner before your own? Were you the distant one, guarding your heart against vulnerability? Understanding these roles can illuminate recurring themes in your love life.

But it's not just about understanding the roles you've played; it's also about recognizing the types of partners you've been drawn to. Often, we find ourselves attracted to the same type of person, repeating cycles without even realizing it. Ask yourself: What traits have my past partners had in common? What dynamics were repeatedly played out in these relationships?

Reflecting on these questions can be enlightening but remember to approach this reflection with kindness and compassion for yourself. The goal is not to assign blame but to gain insight.

Embracing the Present:

One of the most profound lessons in my journey was learning the value of being present. The past is gone, and the future is yet to come. The only real moment we have is now. Embracing the present is a stepping stone to inner peace and a fundamental aspect of self-awareness.

Being present means fully engaging with our current experience, without distraction or escape. It involves tuning into our feelings and thoughts at the moment. This mindfulness allows us to respond to life and relationships more consciously, rather than reacting based on past patterns or future fears.

Start by practicing mindfulness in your daily life. It can be as simple as paying full attention to a routine task, like feeling the water on your hands as you wash dishes, or noticing the sensations in your body as you take a walk. The more you practice being present in your everyday activities, the more you'll bring that presence into your relationships.

Chapter 2: Step Two – Healing

From

Within

"Healing yourself is connected with healing others."

In the journey of love and relationships, healing from within plays a pivotal role. It is often said that we cannot pour from an empty cup, and this rings particularly true when it comes to emotional well-being. In this chapter, we delve into the crucial process of healing from past hurts, fostering self-compassion, and nurturing our emotional health.

Addressing Past Hurts

Healing, a journey often perceived as moving forward, paradoxically requires us to first step back and delve into our past. It's a journey that many of us avoid, for it involves revisiting some of the darkest, most painful chapters of our lives. Yet, it is through this journey that we find the keys to unlock our present and future happiness.

The Nature of Emotional Wounds: Our emotional wounds are often deep-seated and multifaceted. They could stem from a range of experiences – from childhood traumas, such as neglect or abuse, to adult experiences of heartbreak, betrayal, or loss. These wounds might also originate from societal pressures, where constant exposure to unrealistic expectations and norms leaves us feeling inadequate or unfulfilled.

These experiences, particularly those from our formative years, have a profound impact on our psyche. They shape our beliefs about ourselves, others, and the world. For instance, a child who grew up in an environment where love was conditional might develop a belief that they need to earn love and approval constantly. As an adult, this belief might manifest in a pattern of people-pleasing or staying in unfulfilling relationships.

The Challenge of Confrontation: Confronting these wounds requires immense courage. It's not an easy task to face the memories that have caused us so much pain. It might feel like reopening old wounds, but in reality, it's about cleaning those wounds so they can finally heal properly.

During my own journey, I recall the moments I had to revisit painful memories of my past. It was daunting. There were times when the flood of emotions felt overwhelming, and I wanted nothing more than to retreat back into the safety of denial. However, I realized that these emotions were not just obstacles but also signposts, guiding me toward the core issues that needed my attention.

Identifying the Source of Wounds: The first step in addressing these emotional wounds is identifying their source. This process requires honest self-reflection and introspection. It might involve revisiting your childhood memories, past relationships, and significant life events. The aim is not to dwell on these experiences but to understand how they've shaped your current beliefs and behaviors.

For example, think back to your childhood. What was the emotional climate of your home? How did your parents or caregivers express love and affection? Were there experiences of neglect, criticism, or inconsistency? Similarly, reflect on your past relationships. Can you identify patterns in the type of partners you chose or the dynamics that played out in those relationships?

Mindfulness and Meditation: Tools for Healing

One effective method for addressing past hurts is through mindfulness and meditation. These practices help us to connect with our inner selves, offering a space to explore our thoughts and emotions without judgment.

Mindfulness Practice: Begin by finding a quiet place where you can sit comfortably without distractions. Close your eyes and take deep, slow breaths. Focus on your breath, noticing the sensations in your body. As you settle into this state of calmness, allow memories and emotions to surface naturally. Observe these thoughts and feelings without judgment or attachment. Acknowledge their presence and gently bring your focus back to your breath.

This practice helps create a safe space for your emotions, allowing you to confront your past hurts in a controlled and mindful environment. The key lies in learning to observe your emotional responses without being overwhelmed by them.

Guided Meditation for Healing: Set aside some time for this guided meditation. Sit or lie down in a comfortable position and close your eyes. Take a few deep breaths to center yourself. Imagine a safe, peaceful place - it could be a garden, a beach, or any place where you feel calm and secure.

Visualize yourself in this safe space. As you relax, allow memories of past hurts to come to the forefront of your mind. Visualize these memories as objects - perhaps as stones or leaves floating in a stream. Acknowledge each memory, each emotion associated with it, and then visualize placing it in the stream. Watch as the stream carries it away, symbolizing your release of its hold over you.

As you progress through this exercise, remind yourself that you are safe and in control. You are not your past; you are a person with the strength and resilience to heal and move forward.

As you embark on this journey of confronting your past, it's important to navigate through the pain with care and compassion. Healing is not a linear process; it's normal to have days where you feel you've made significant progress and others where you feel stuck. If at any point the process becomes too overwhelming, it's okay to step back and take a break. Healing should not be rushed. It's a process that unfolds in its own time. Be gentle with yourself and acknowledge the courage it takes to face your past.

The Light at the End of the Tunnel

Despite the challenges, confronting our past hurts is a profoundly liberating experience. Each layer of pain you peel back brings you closer to your true self – the self that is not defined by past wounds but by the strength and wisdom gained from healing them.

In my journey, every memory I revisited, every emotion I allowed myself to feel brought me a step closer to freedom. With each revelation, I found pieces of myself that I had lost along the way. I learned to forgive, not just others, but also myself. I discovered a wellspring of resilience and self-compassion that I didn't know existed within me.

Addressing past hurts is a crucial step in the journey toward self-awareness and healing. It's a path that leads us not only to a deeper understanding of ourselves but also opens the door to more genuine, fulfilling relationships. In the next sections, we will explore how to foster self-compassion and nurture our emotional health, further enhancing our ability to love and be loved.

Fostering Self-Compassion

Fostering self-compassion transcends being just a self-help strategy; it represents a fundamental shift in how we engage with ourselves. Transforming the internal script from self-criticism and doubt to one of support and belief is essential. This internal transformation plays a crucial role in healing past wounds and preventing new ones from forming.

The Essence of Self-Compassion: This practice embodies the art of being your own ally. Recognizing our human fallibility and worthiness of kindness, we understand that mistakes and flaws are part of the universal human experience. By treating ourselves as we would a good friend, we unlock a profound source of comfort and healing.

This shift can be challenging, especially if self-criticism has been our go-to response. It's a habit that's reinforced over years or even decades, and changing it requires a consistent and conscious effort. But the benefits are manifold – research has shown that self-compassion leads to greater emotional resilience, increased happiness, and a better quality of life.

Sounds fancy, but it's really just about being nice to yourself. And believe me, it's not always easy. I've stumbled through this myself, tripping over old habits of being my own worst critic. But here's the thing – it gets better. Every kind word you throw your way is like a high-five to your heart. As you dive in keep in mind, I've been right where you are, and I made it through. You've got this. And remember, it's all about taking it one step, one high-five at a time.

Shifting the Internal Dialogue: Our internal dialogue can be our harshest critic or our greatest supporter. It's often a reflection of how we were spoken to during our formative years, but the beauty lies in our ability to reshape it as adults. The process begins with awareness – noticing when our inner voice is slipping into patterns of criticism and negativity.

When we catch ourselves in a cycle of self-criticism, it's crucial to pause and take a step back. Ask yourself, "Would I speak to someone I care about in this way?" If the answer is no, then it's a clear sign that your inner dialogue needs to be shifted.

Practicing Self-Compassion Through Affirmations: Daily affirmations are a practical and effective way to practice self-compassion. These are positive, first-person statements that you repeat to yourself, designed to challenge negative beliefs and reinforce a compassionate self-view.

Here's a step-by-step guide to creating and practicing daily affirmations:

1. Identify Negative Self-Talk: Pay attention to the themes of your self-criticism. Is it about your appearance, intelligence, worthiness, or something else?

2. Create Affirmations: For each theme of self-criticism, create an affirmation that counters the negative belief. If you criticize your intelligence, your affirmation might be, "I am intelligent and capable of learning from my experiences."

3. Integrate Emotion: The most effective affirmations are those that evoke a positive emotional response. They don't just challenge negative beliefs; they make you feel good when you say them.

4. Daily Practice: Set aside time each morning to repeat your affirmations. Say them out loud, write them down, or even say them to yourself in the mirror. Make it a ritual – a moment of self-connection.

5. Use Affirmations Reactively: When you notice negative self-talk, pause and use your affirmations to reframe your

thoughts. This can help stop the spiral of self-criticism in its tracks.

6. Reinforcement Throughout the Day: Keep your affirmations visible – as a note on your phone, a post-it on your mirror, or even a reminder in your calendar. The more you reinforce the message, the more ingrained it will become.

Affirmations in Action: Let's say you've made a mistake at work, and the familiar voice of self-criticism starts its chorus of, "You're not good enough." This is the moment to employ your affirmations. You might say to yourself, "I am competent and learn from my mistakes," or, "I am growing and improving every day."

Fostering self-compassion is akin to learning a new language—the language of kindness directed inward. As you practice this gentle form of self-communication, you reinforce the understanding that you are worthy of love and respect, just as you are. Here are additional affirmations to incorporate into your daily practice, each designed to bolster your self-esteem and fortify your self-compassion:

- "I am deserving of happiness and love."

- "I accept myself unconditionally."

- "I am full of potential and my possibilities are endless."

- "I honor my own life path and respect my own pace."

- "I am strong, resilient, and equipped to handle life's challenges."

- "I embrace my imperfections as part of my unique beauty."

- "I give myself permission to grow and to rest, as needed."

- "My challenges do not define me; they refine me."

- "I am a work of art, ever-evolving and inherently valuable."

Remember, affirmations are not just phrases you recite; they are declarations of your commitment to treat yourself with more kindness and less judgment.

Compassion in Reflection

Self-compassion also involves looking back at your past with kindness. Instead of berating yourself for past actions, view them with understanding. Recognize that you did the best you could with the knowledge and skills you had at the time.

Developing a Compassionate Response: Developing a compassionate inner voice is a skill that takes time. It might feel awkward or forced at first, but with practice, it becomes a natural part of your thought process. Here are some ways to cultivate that compassionate response:

- Mindfulness Meditation: Spend a few minutes each day in meditation, focusing on cultivating feelings of self-compassion. Imagine sending love and kindness to yourself, perhaps visualizing it as a warm light surrounding you.

- Self-Compassion Breaks: When you're feeling overwhelmed or critical, take a short break. Place a hand over your heart, take deep breaths, and offer yourself some kind words.

- Gratitude: At the end of each day, reflect on three things you are grateful for about yourself. This practice can help shift the focus from criticism to appreciation.

Fostering self-compassion is an ongoing journey, one that has the power to transform not only how you view yourself but also how you engage with the world. As you become more compassionate towards yourself, you'll notice a ripple effect in your relationships. You'll approach others with more understanding and kindness, further enriching your connections.

Nurturing Your Emotional Health

Emotional health is the unsung hero of our well-being. It's the quiet engine that powers our daily experiences and shapes our interactions. To nurture our emotional health is to attend to the garden of our inner landscape, ensuring that it's cared for with the same diligence we give to our physical selves.

To cultivate a thriving emotional landscape, consider these five foundational aspects of emotional health:

1. Mindful Awareness: Just as a gardener must be aware of the needs of each plant, we must become mindful of our emotional states. Recognizing and acknowledging our feelings without judgment is the first step to understanding and managing them effectively.

2. Positive Environment: Our surroundings can influence our emotional state. Aim to create a living space that is a reflection of calm and inspiration. This can be as simple as keeping your area tidy, letting in natural light, or decorating with items that bring you joy.

3. Healthy Relationships: The company we keep can either

nourish or deplete our emotional well-being. Cultivate relationships that are supportive and uplifting, and learn to set boundaries with those that drain your emotional energy.

4. Self-Care Rituals: Incorporate regular activities into your life that promote relaxation and joy. This could be a daily routine, like sipping a morning cup of tea in silence, which serves as an anchor of tranquility.

5. Expressive Outlets: Find creative ways to express your emotions. Whether through art, writing, music, or dance, expressing yourself is a therapeutic way to work through complex feelings and foster emotional growth.

Mindful Awareness: To truly nurture our emotional health, we need to start with mindful awareness. Think of it like this: just as a gardener needs to be aware of the slightest changes in their garden, we need to be in tune with our inner world. Being mindfully aware means noticing our feelings—the flutter of joy at a child's laughter, the surge of irritation in a traffic jam, or the swell of sadness from an old song. It's not about changing these feelings but noticing them, naming them, and understanding where they come from.

Mindful awareness is about living in the 'now'. It's easy to get lost in regrets of the past or worries about the future, but life is happening in the present moment. When we're mindful, we're fully engaged in what we're doing, whether it's eating a meal, having a conversation, or even doing chores.

Practical Practices for Cultivating Mindful Awareness

In the whirlwind of daily life, with its incessant demands and relentless pace, I discovered something vital: mindfulness need not be a luxury or a drawn-out ritual; it can be woven into the fabric of our everyday existence. This revelation didn't come from a place of tranquility but from necessity — the need to find calm in the chaos of a schedule that never seemed to let up.

For my fellow busy bees out there, I've distilled the essence of mindfulness into five simple practices that I personally crafted and folded into the nooks and crannies of my own jam-packed days. Each one is a thread in the tapestry of a balanced life, designed not to overwhelm but to integrate smoothly into our routines. They are concise yet powerful brief interludes that collectively maintain our emotional equilibrium, even as we dash from task to task.

Let me guide you through these practices. Each one is a stepping stone that I laid down on my journey, helping me to navigate the bustling river of life without getting swept away. They have been my anchors, and I am excited to share them with you, hoping they will become yours too. These are the practices that can bring us back to ourselves, ensuring that we don't just go through our days but actually grow through them.

1. Micro-Meditations: In the rush of a busy day, it can be hard to spare even five minutes for meditation. Instead, try micro-meditations. Multiple times throughout your day, take just 30 seconds to close your eyes and focus on your breath. Inhale deeply, then exhale slowly, letting the brief pause re-center your thoughts. You can do this between meetings, while waiting for your coffee to brew, or after checking emails. Over time, these half-minute meditations can accu-

mulate to create a profound sense of calm and focus.

2. Mindful Sips: Transform your coffee break into a session of mindfulness. Instead of drinking your coffee on the go, take a moment to hold the cup, feel its warmth, and inhale the aroma. Sip slowly, savoring each taste and noticing how it feels as you drink. Allow this to be a deliberate pause in your day, a time when you're fully present with your coffee. This practice can be a daily ritual that not only energizes your body but also calms your mind.

3. Conscious Commuting: Use your commute as an opportunity for mindfulness. If you're driving, notice the grip of your hands on the steering wheel, the scenery passing by, the rhythm of traffic. If you're a passenger, listen to the sounds around you, feel the movement, and observe your thoughts without getting attached to them. This can turn a potentially stressful commute into valuable "me time."

4. Responsive Relaxation: The body scan technique can be adapted for a busy lifestyle. While seated at your desk or during a short break, take a moment to tune into your body. Start with your feet, feeling any sensations, and work your way up to your head. It can be done in as little as two minutes. This quick check-in helps release any built-up tension and brings a greater awareness of the mind-body connection.

5. Active Appreciation: Gratitude doesn't require a journal; it can be a mental note. Throughout your day, acknowledge moments you're thankful for. It could be a meaningful conversation, a helpful colleague, or the sunset during your

ride home. These mental acknowledgments of gratitude can shift your perspective, turning everyday occurrences into a series of appreciated moments and enriching your day with positivity.

Integrating these five practices into your daily routine paves the way for a mindful awareness that bolsters emotional health, seamlessly fitting into your busy schedule. These practices hinge on subtle changes in your approach to everyday activities

As you practice these simple exercises, you become more attuned to your emotional landscape. Like the vigilant gardener who knows the state of their garden by the feel of the soil and the look of the leaves, you'll come to know the state of your inner world with clarity and understanding. you may find that your sense of peace and emotional well-being grows. You might notice that you're less reactive, more patient, and more present in your relationships. This is the power of mindful awareness – it transforms not just your inner world but also how you interact with the world around you.

Remember, the goal of mindful awareness is not to empty your mind or escape your emotions but to experience them fully, without judgment or criticism. This process involves developing a friendly curiosity towards your inner experiences, learning to be with them, understanding them, and, ultimately, gaining insight into your own nature.

Positive Environment: In the rush and tumble of our daily grind, where every tick of the clock seems to demand action, it's easy to forget the subtle ways our environment impacts us. I learned that the hard way—in the midst of chaos, when my soul was crying out for a breath of peace. That's when I realized that our spaces are not just places;

they're sanctuaries for our emotions, canvases for our moods. So I set out to transform my own space, and in doing so, I uncovered simple, transformative practices that anyone, no matter how packed their schedule, could benefit from. Here's how you can create a positive environment in three manageable steps:

1. Tidy Up in Ten - The Quick-Fix Cleanse: Your living space is the stage for your daily life. A clean and inviting stage sets the tone for your performance. The 'Tidy Up in Ten' approach is akin to a speed-cleaning session – it's quick, effective, and surprisingly fulfilling. Set a timer for ten minutes and see how much you can accomplish. This isn't about a thorough overhaul, but about daily maintenance; a challenge to beat yesterday's effort in decluttering or organizing. Turn on some music to make it enjoyable. Just last week, during one of these sessions, a friend discovered a treasured item they thought was lost forever – a reminder of the unexpected joys of tidying up.

2. Embrace the Light - Bask in Your Personal Sunshine: The presence of natural light can significantly affect your mood and energy levels. If your workspace feels like a gloomy cave, consider moving it closer to a source of natural light. A colleague of mine, for instance, replaced the lighting around his desk with a daylight simulation bulb. The transformation in his mood and productivity was remarkable. For those working in less-than-ideal lighting conditions, light therapy lamps can be an effective solution, providing a semblance of natural sunlight that can uplift your spirits and enhance your workspace.

3. Personalize Your Peace - Curate Your Joy Gallery: This step is about turning your space into a personal haven of happiness. It involves surrounding yourself with objects that bring you joy and comfort. For example, a friend of mine has adorned her workspace with a collection of items that hold special meaning for her: a coffee mug from a memorable vacation, a small indoor plant that adds a touch of greenery, and a calendar filled with inspiring quotes. Each of these items serves as a joyful reminder, a small yet significant touch that brightens her day. Think of your space as a gallery of personal delights, each item a reflection of what brings you happiness and serenity amidst the hustle of daily life.

By following these simple steps, you can transform your surroundings into a more positive and uplifting environment, enhancing your well-being and productivity.

Healthy Relationships: In the sprint of our daily routines, where every minute is accounted for, the people we interact with can either be a dose of energy or a drain. Trust me, I'm right there with you. My days are a blur of meetings, messages, and mile-long to-do lists. That's why I love simplicity, and I stick to concepts that don't need a manual to be understood. It's from my own hit-and-miss adventures with people that I've learned how crucial it is to have relationships that don't feel like another job.

So, let's talk real talk, from one busy person to another. I've put together a list of five straightforward, tried-and-true ways to cultivate relationships that add value to our lives, not stress. These aren't just theories; they're the actual strategies I use to keep my emotional health in check while juggling the chaos of a packed schedule. Here they are:

Step Two – Healing From Whitin

♥

"Healing yourself is connected with healing others."

In the journey of love and relationships, healing from within plays a pivotal role. It is often said that we cannot pour from an empty cup, and this rings particularly true when it comes to emotional well-being. In this chapter, we delve into the crucial process of healing from past hurts, fostering self-compassion, and nurturing our emotional health.

Addressing Past Hurts:

Healing, a journey often perceived as moving forward, paradoxically requires us to first step back and delve into our past. It's a journey that many of us avoid, for it involves revisiting some of the darkest, most painful chapters of our lives. Yet, it is through this journey that we find the keys to unlock our present and future happiness.

The Nature of Emotional Wounds: Our emotional wounds are often deep-seated and multifaceted. They could stem from a range of experiences – from childhood traumas, such as neglect or abuse, to adult experiences of heartbreak, betrayal, or loss. These wounds might also originate from societal pressures, where constant exposure to unrealistic expectations and norms leaves us feeling inadequate or unfulfilled.

These experiences, particularly those from our formative years, have a profound impact on our psyche. They shape our beliefs about ourselves, others, and the world. For instance, a child who grew up in an environment where love was conditional might develop a belief that they need to earn love and approval constantly. As an adult, this belief might manifest in a pattern of people-pleasing or staying in unfulfilling relationships.

The Challenge of Confrontation: Confronting these wounds requires immense courage. It's not an easy task to face the memories that have caused us so much pain. It might feel like reopening old wounds, but in reality, it's about cleaning those wounds so they can finally heal properly.

During my own journey, I recall the moments I had to revisit painful memories of my past. It was daunting. There were times when the flood of emotions felt overwhelming, and I wanted nothing more than to retreat back into the safety of denial. However, I realized that these emotions were not just obstacles but also signposts, guiding me toward the core issues that needed my attention.

Identifying the Source of Wounds: The first step in addressing these emotional wounds is identifying their source. This process requires honest self-reflection and introspection. It might involve revisiting your childhood memories, past relationships, and significant life events. The aim is not to dwell on these experiences but to understand how they've shaped your current beliefs and behaviors.

For example, think back to your childhood. What was the emotional climate of your home? How did your parents or caregivers express love and affection? Were there experiences of neglect, criticism, or inconsistency? Similarly, reflect on your past relationships. Can you identify patterns in the type of partners you chose or the dynamics that played out in those relationships?

Mindfulness and Meditation: Tools for Healing

One effective method for addressing past hurts is through mindfulness and meditation. These practices help us to connect with our inner selves, offering a space to explore our thoughts and emotions without judgment.

Mindfulness Practice: Begin by finding a quiet place where you can sit comfortably without distractions. Close your eyes and take deep, slow breaths. Focus on your breath, noticing the sensations in your body. As you settle into this state of calmness, allow memories and emotions to surface naturally. Observe these thoughts and feelings without judgment or attachment. Acknowledge their presence and gently bring your focus back to your breath.

This practice helps create a safe space for your emotions, allowing you to confront your past hurts in a controlled and mindful environment. The key lies in learning to observe your emotional responses without being overwhelmed by them.

Guided Meditation for Healing: Set aside some time for this guided meditation. Sit or lie down in a comfortable position and close your eyes. Take a few deep breaths to center yourself. Imagine a safe, peaceful place - it could be a garden, a beach, or any place where you feel calm and secure.

Visualize yourself in this safe space. As you relax, allow memories of past hurts to come to the forefront of your mind. Visualize these memories as objects - perhaps as stones or leaves floating in a stream. Acknowledge each memory, each emotion associated with it, and then visualize placing it in the stream. Watch as the stream carries it away, symbolizing your release of its hold over you.

As you progress through this exercise, remind yourself that you are safe and in control. You are not your past; you are a person with the strength and resilience to heal and move forward.

As you embark on this journey of confronting your past, it's important to navigate through the pain with care and compassion. Healing is not a linear process; it's normal to have days where you feel you've made significant progress and others where you feel stuck. If at any point the process becomes too overwhelming, it's okay to step back and take a break. Healing should not be rushed. It's a process that unfolds in its own time. Be gentle with yourself and acknowledge the courage it takes to face your past.

The Light at the End of the Tunnel:

Despite the challenges, confronting our past hurts is a profoundly liberating experience. Each layer of pain you peel back brings you closer to your true self – the self that is not defined by past wounds but by the strength and wisdom gained from healing them.

In my journey, every memory I revisited, every emotion I allowed myself to feel brought me a step closer to freedom. With each revelation, I found pieces of myself that I had lost along the way. I learned to forgive, not just others, but also myself. I discovered a wellspring of resilience and self-compassion that I didn't know existed within me.

Addressing past hurts is a crucial step in the journey toward self-awareness and healing. It's a path that leads us not only to a deeper understanding of ourselves but also opens the door to more genuine, fulfilling relationships. In the next sections, we will explore how to foster self-compassion and nurture our emotional health, further enhancing our ability to love and be loved.

Fostering Self-Compassion:

Fostering self-compassion transcends being just a self-help strategy; it represents a fundamental shift in how we engage with ourselves. Transforming the internal script from self-criticism and doubt to one of support and belief is essential. This internal transformation plays a crucial role in healing past wounds and preventing new ones from forming.

The Essence of Self-Compassion: This practice embodies the art of being your own ally. Recognizing our human fallibility and worthiness of kindness, we understand that mistakes and flaws are part of the universal human experience. By treating ourselves as we would a good friend, we unlock a profound source of comfort and healing.

This shift can be challenging, especially if self-criticism has been our go-to response. It's a habit that's reinforced over years or even decades, and changing it requires a consistent and conscious effort. But the benefits are manifold – research has shown that self-compassion leads to greater emotional resilience, increased happiness, and a better quality of life.

Sounds fancy, but it's really just about being nice to yourself. And believe me, it's not always easy. I've stumbled through this myself, tripping over old habits of being my own worst critic. But here's the thing – it gets better. Every kind word you throw your way is like a high-five to your heart. As you dive in keep in mind, I've been right where you are, and I made it through. You've got this. And remember, it's all about taking it one step, one high-five at a time.

Shifting the Internal Dialogue: Our internal dialogue can be our harshest critic or our greatest supporter. It's often a reflection of how we were spoken to during our formative years, but the beauty lies in our ability to reshape it as adults. The process begins with awareness – noticing when our inner voice is slipping into patterns of criticism and negativity.

When we catch ourselves in a cycle of self-criticism, it's crucial to pause and take a step back. Ask yourself, "Would I speak to someone I care about in this way?" If the answer is no, then it's a clear sign that your inner dialogue needs to be shifted.

Practicing Self-Compassion Through Affirmations: Daily affirmations are a practical and effective way to practice self-compassion. These are positive, first-person statements that you repeat to yourself, designed to challenge negative beliefs and reinforce a compassionate self-view.

Here's a step-by-step guide to creating and practicing daily affirmations:

1. Identify Negative Self-Talk: Pay attention to the themes of your self-criticism. Is it about your appearance, intelligence, worthiness, or something else?

2. Create Affirmations: For each theme of self-criticism, create an affirmation that counters the negative belief. If you criticize your intelligence, your affirmation might be, "I am intelligent and capable of learning from my experiences."

3. Integrate Emotion: The most effective affirmations are those that evoke a positive emotional response. They don't just challenge negative beliefs; they make you feel good when you say them.

4. Daily Practice: Set aside time each morning to repeat your affirmations. Say them out loud, write them down, or even say them to yourself in the mirror. Make it a ritual – a moment of self-connection.

5. Use Affirmations Reactively: When you notice negative self-talk, pause and use your affirmations to reframe your thoughts. This can help stop the spiral of self-criticism in its tracks.

6. Reinforcement Throughout the Day: Keep your affirmations visible – as a note on your phone, a post-it on your mirror, or even a reminder in your calendar. The more you reinforce the message, the more ingrained it will become.

Affirmations in Action: Let's say you've made a mistake at work, and the familiar voice of self-criticism starts its chorus of, "You're not good enough." This is the moment to employ your affirmations. You might say to yourself, "I am competent and learn from my mistakes," or, "I am growing and improving every day."

Fostering self-compassion is akin to learning a new language—the language of kindness directed inward. As you practice this gentle form of self-communication, you reinforce the understanding that you are worthy of love and respect, just as you are. Here are additional affirmations to incorporate into your daily practice, each designed to bolster your self-esteem and fortify your self-compassion:

- "I am deserving of happiness and love."

- "I accept myself unconditionally."

- "I am full of potential and my possibilities are endless."

- "I honor my own life path and respect my own pace."

- "I am strong, resilient, and equipped to handle life's challenges."

- "I embrace my imperfections as part of my unique beauty."

- "I give myself permission to grow and to rest, as needed."

- "My challenges do not define me; they refine me."

- "I am a work of art, ever-evolving and inherently valuable."

Remember, affirmations are not just phrases you recite; they are declarations of your commitment to treat yourself with more kindness and less judgment.

Compassion in Reflection:

Self-compassion also involves looking back at your past with kindness. Instead of berating yourself for past actions, view them with understanding. Recognize that you did the best you could with the knowledge and skills you had at the time.

Developing a Compassionate Response: Developing a compassionate inner voice is a skill that takes time. It might feel awkward or forced at first, but with practice, it becomes a natural part of your thought process. Here are some ways to cultivate that compassionate response:

- Mindfulness Meditation: Spend a few minutes each day in meditation, focusing on cultivating feelings of self-compassion. Imagine sending love and kindness to yourself, perhaps visualizing it as a warm light surrounding you.

- Self-Compassion Breaks: When you're feeling overwhelmed or critical, take a short break. Place a hand over your heart, take deep breaths, and offer yourself some kind words.

- Gratitude: At the end of each day, reflect on three things you are grateful for about yourself. This practice can help shift the focus from criticism to appreciation.

Fostering self-compassion is an ongoing journey, one that has the power to transform not only how you view yourself but also how you engage with the world. As you become more compassionate towards yourself, you'll notice a ripple effect in your relationships. You'll approach others with more understanding and kindness, further enriching your connections.

Nurturing Your Emotional Health:

Emotional health is the unsung hero of our well-being. It's the quiet engine that powers our daily experiences and shapes our interactions. To nurture our emotional health is to attend to the garden of our inner landscape, ensuring that it's cared for with the same diligence we give to our physical selves.

To cultivate a thriving emotional landscape, consider these five foundational aspects of emotional health:

1. Mindful Awareness: Just as a gardener must be aware of the needs of each plant, we must become mindful of our emotional states. Recognizing and acknowledging our feelings without judgment is the first step to understanding and managing them effectively.

2. Positive Environment: Our surroundings can influence our emotional state. Aim to create a living space that is a reflection of calm and inspiration. This can be as simple as keeping your area tidy, letting in natural light, or decorating with items that bring you joy.

3. Healthy Relationships: The company we keep can either nourish or deplete our emotional well-being. Cultivate relationships that are supportive and uplifting, and learn to set boundaries with those that drain your emotional energy.

4. Self-Care Rituals: Incorporate regular activities into your life that promote relaxation and joy. This could be a daily routine, like sipping a morning cup of tea in silence, which serves as an anchor of tranquility.

5. Expressive Outlets: Find creative ways to express your emo-

tions. Whether through art, writing, music, or dance, expressing yourself is a therapeutic way to work through complex feelings and foster emotional growth.

Mindful Awareness: To truly nurture our emotional health, we need to start with mindful awareness. Think of it like this: just as a gardener needs to be aware of the slightest changes in their garden, we need to be in tune with our inner world. Being mindfully aware means noticing our feelings—the flutter of joy at a child's laughter, the surge of irritation in a traffic jam, or the swell of sadness from an old song. It's not about changing these feelings but noticing them, naming them, and understanding where they come from.

Mindful awareness is about living in the 'now'. It's easy to get lost in regrets of the past or worries about the future, but life is happening in the present moment. When we're mindful, we're fully engaged in what we're doing, whether it's eating a meal, having a conversation, or even doing chores.

Practical Practices for Cultivating Mindful Awareness:

In the whirlwind of daily life, with its incessant demands and relentless pace, I discovered something vital: mindfulness need not be a luxury or a drawn-out ritual; it can be woven into the fabric of our everyday existence. This revelation didn't come from a place of tranquility but from necessity — the need to find calm in the chaos of a schedule that never seemed to let up.

For my fellow busy bees out there, I've distilled the essence of mindfulness into five simple practices that I personally crafted and folded into the nooks and crannies of my own jam-packed days. Each one is a thread in the tapestry of a balanced life, designed not to overwhelm but to integrate smoothly into our routines. They are concise yet powerful brief interludes that collectively maintain our emotional equilibrium, even as we dash from task to task.

Let me guide you through these practices. Each one is a stepping stone that I laid down on my journey, helping me to navigate the bustling river of life without getting swept away. They have been my anchors, and I am excited to share them with you, hoping they will become yours too. These are the practices that can bring us back to ourselves, ensuring that we don't just go through our days but actually grow through them.

1. Micro-Meditations: In the rush of a busy day, it can be hard to spare even five minutes for meditation. Instead, try micro-meditations. Multiple times throughout your day, take just 30 seconds to close your eyes and focus on your breath. Inhale deeply, then exhale slowly, letting the brief pause re-center your thoughts. You can do this between meetings, while waiting for your coffee to brew, or after checking emails. Over time, these half-minute meditations can accumulate to create a profound sense of calm and focus.

2. Mindful Sips: Transform your coffee break into a session of mindfulness. Instead of drinking your coffee on the go, take a moment to hold the cup, feel its warmth, and inhale the aroma. Sip slowly, savoring each taste and noticing how it feels as you drink. Allow this to be a deliberate pause in your day, a time when you're fully present with your coffee. This practice can be a daily ritual that not only energizes your body but also calms your mind.

3. Conscious Commuting: Use your commute as an opportunity for mindfulness. If you're driving, notice the grip of your hands on the steering wheel, the scenery passing by, the rhythm of traffic. If you're a passenger, listen to the sounds around you, feel the movement, and observe your thoughts without getting attached to them. This can turn a potentially stressful commute into valuable "me time."

4. Responsive Relaxation: The body scan technique can be adapted for a busy lifestyle. While seated at your desk or during a short break, take a moment to tune into your body. Start with your feet, feeling any sensations, and work your way up to your head. It can be done in as little as two minutes. This quick check-in helps release any built-up tension and brings a greater awareness of the mind-body connection.

5. Active Appreciation: Gratitude doesn't require a journal; it can be a mental note. Throughout your day, acknowledge moments you're thankful for. It could be a meaningful conversation, a helpful colleague, or the sunset during your ride home. These mental acknowledgments of gratitude can shift your perspective, turning everyday occurrences into a series of appreciated moments and enriching your day with positivity.

Integrating these five practices into your daily routine paves the way for a mindful awareness that bolsters emotional health, seamlessly fitting into your busy schedule. These practices hinge on subtle changes in your approach to everyday activities

As you practice these simple exercises, you become more attuned to your emotional landscape. Like the vigilant gardener who knows the state of their garden by the feel of the soil and the look of the leaves, you'll come to know the state of your inner world with clarity and understanding. you may find that your sense of peace and emotional well-being grows. You might notice that you're less reactive, more patient, and more present in your relationships. This is the power of mindful awareness – it transforms not just your inner world but also how you interact with the world around you.

Remember, the goal of mindful awareness is not to empty your mind or escape your emotions but to experience them fully, without judgment or criticism. This process involves developing a friendly curiosity towards your inner experiences, learning to be with them, understanding them, and, ultimately, gaining insight into your own nature.

Positive Environment: In the rush and tumble of our daily grind, where every tick of the clock seems to demand action, it's easy to forget the subtle ways our environment impacts us. I learned that the hard way—in the midst of chaos, when my soul was crying out for a breath of peace. That's when I realized that our spaces are not just places; they're sanctuaries for our emotions, canvases for our moods. So I set out to transform my own space, and in doing so, I uncovered simple, transformative practices that anyone, no matter how packed their schedule, could benefit from. Here's how you can create a positive environment in three manageable steps:

> 1. Tidy Up in Ten - The Quick-Fix Cleanse: Your living space is the stage for your daily life. A clean and inviting stage sets the tone for your performance. The 'Tidy Up in Ten' approach is akin to a speed-cleaning session – it's quick, effective, and

surprisingly fulfilling. Set a timer for ten minutes and see how much you can accomplish. This isn't about a thorough overhaul, but about daily maintenance; a challenge to beat yesterday's effort in decluttering or organizing. Turn on some music to make it enjoyable. Just last week, during one of these sessions, a friend discovered a treasured item they thought was lost forever – a reminder of the unexpected joys of tidying up.

2. Embrace the Light - Bask in Your Personal Sunshine: The presence of natural light can significantly affect your mood and energy levels. If your workspace feels like a gloomy cave, consider moving it closer to a source of natural light. A colleague of mine, for instance, replaced the lighting around his desk with a daylight simulation bulb. The transformation in his mood and productivity was remarkable. For those working in less-than-ideal lighting conditions, light therapy lamps can be an effective solution, providing a semblance of natural sunlight that can uplift your spirits and enhance your workspace.

3. Personalize Your Peace - Curate Your Joy Gallery: This step is about turning your space into a personal haven of happiness. It involves surrounding yourself with objects that bring you joy and comfort. For example, a friend of mine has adorned her workspace with a collection of items that hold special meaning for her: a coffee mug from a memorable vacation, a small indoor plant that adds a touch of greenery, and a calendar filled with inspiring quotes. Each of these items serves as a joyful reminder, a small yet significant touch that brightens her day. Think of your space as a gallery of personal

delights, each item a reflection of what brings you happiness and serenity amidst the hustle of daily life.

By following these simple steps, you can transform your surroundings into a more positive and uplifting environment, enhancing your well-being and productivity.

Healthy Relationships:

In the sprint of our daily routines, where every minute is accounted for, the people we interact with can either be a dose of energy or a drain. Trust me, I'm right there with you. My days are a blur of meetings, messages, and mile-long to-do lists. That's why I love simplicity, and I stick to concepts that don't need a manual to be understood. It's from my own hit-and-miss adventures with people that I've learned how crucial it is to have relationships that don't feel like another job.

So, let's talk real talk, from one busy person to another. I've put together a list of five straightforward, tried-and-true ways to cultivate relationships that add value to our lives, not stress. These aren't just theories; they're the actual strategies I use to keep my emotional health in check while juggling the chaos of a packed schedule. Here they are:

1. The 'Good Vibes' Filter: Think of your social interactions like a carefully curated playlist where each person's energy contributes to the overall vibe. Consider Dave, my co-worker, whose passion for his startup is so infectious that it turns even a mundane coffee break into an inspiring brainstorming session. His enthusiasm acts as a catalyst, motivating everyone around him, including me, to think more innovatively. Then there's Mia, a long-time friend whose serene presence is like a breath of fresh air in the chaos of everyday life. Her

ability to remain calm and centered, even in stressful situations, teaches me the value of patience and resilience. The key here is recognizing these positive influences and intentionally spending more time with people who uplift and energize you, just like the songs that never fail to lift your spirits.

2. Energy Checkpoints: Your energy levels are a great indicator of the impact your social interactions have on you. For example, post-lunch meetings with my colleague Mark often left me feeling depleted, his pessimism acting like a drain on my enthusiasm. Recognizing this, I started to limit our one-on-one meetings and instead focused on team meetings where the collective energy was more balanced and positive. This small change not only conserved my energy but also allowed me to contribute more effectively in a group setting. Similarly, reassessing your interactions and adjusting them to maintain a healthy energy balance is crucial for long-term well-being and productivity.

3. Firm Lines, Kind Words: Setting boundaries is essential for healthy relationships, but it's important to do so with empathy and kindness. My neighbor Laura, who loves spontaneity, often dropped by unannounced, which could be overwhelming at times. By gently expressing my need for planned interactions, saying, "Laura, I really value our time together, but I find I can enjoy it more when we schedule it in advance," helped set a respectful boundary. This approach acknowledges her desire for spontaneous connection while also honoring my need for a more structured schedule, fostering mutual respect and understanding in our friendship.

4. The Power of Presence: In a world where distractions are the norm, being fully present in social interactions is a gift. When having dinner with my friend Alex, I made a conscious effort to put my phone away and listen actively. This shift in behavior not only deepened our conversation but also strengthened our friendship, as Alex felt genuinely heard and valued. Such undivided attention can transform casual meetups into meaningful experiences, enriching both your life and those of your friends.

5. Mirror Moments: Reflecting on how you interact with friends and striving to balance giving and receiving support is crucial. I realized I was always the one trying to uplift my friends but seldom allowed them space to do the same for me. When I consciously started asking my friend Sarah about her day and actively listening to her, it not only helped me understand her better but also strengthened our bond. Being a good friend means being there for others as much as they are there for you, and sometimes that means stepping back and letting them shine.

These practices aren't just bullet points on a list; they're strategies for a more fulfilled life. By applying them, you'll find that your relationships are less about filling time and more about enriching your life, and theirs, one interaction at a time.

Self-Care Rituals:

I've always been one to ride life's fast lane — always moving, always hustling. But even race cars need pit stops. I realized I had to create pockets of reprieve that could seamlessly blend into my high-speed days. That's why I engineered these five self-care rituals, not from a place of leisure, but from necessity and through trial and error. They're born from those tiny gaps in a schedule that's packed tighter than a subway at rush hour, and designed for the real world where time is the most precious commodity.

The first ritual came to me on a morning that felt particularly grueling. I needed a jolt stronger than caffeine and less jarring than an alarm. The answer? A cold shower. It started as a dare from a friend but quickly became my secret weapon. Two minutes under the chill, and I'm more awake than any espresso could ever make me. It's not just about the cold; it's about starting the day with a challenge already conquered.

Then there was the daily commute, my personal time eater. I was already a captive audience to my steering wheel, so why not make it count? Podcasts became my portal to new worlds, ideas, and inspirations. Every traffic jam was no longer a frustration but an opportunity to explore a new episode. And as for those moments in between meetings and emails, I developed 'deskercise' routines — nothing like a few incognito stretches and stealthy squats to keep the energy flowing.

Evenings, once a blur of blue screens, are now my no-screen wind-down. That's my signal that the day is done, and the digital world can wait. This shift isn't rooted in grand gestures of self-care; it centers on the little things that affirm, 'Hey, you're doing alright.' These practices are more than mere actions; they're affirmations — small declarations that, even amidst the chaos, I haven't forgotten the person at the helm: me. So, if your life feels perpetually stuck in fifth gear, consider integrating these rituals. They might just transform into the essential pit stops that keep your engine running smoothly and sustainably.

Life's a non-stop merry-go-round, and let me tell you, the dizzying speed doesn't always come with a thrill. I needed something real, something that could stick, and here's what I found:

1. The Two-Minute Cold Shower: Once upon a bleary-eyed morning, my trusty coffee pot failed to work its magic. Desperate times called for desperate measures, and so the cold shower became my new ritual. At first, it was a shock, a gasp-inducing plunge into icy waters. But then something clicked. It became my battle cry against the drowsiness, a physical declaration that I was awake, alive, and not just going through the motions. And you know what? If I can conquer the cold at dawn, what's a day's worth of challenges? Try it. Let the cold be your herald of a day where you're the hero from the start.

2. The Commute Podcast: The daily commute was my 'lost time,' until I transformed it into my 'found time.' Podcasts became my gateway to adventure, learning, and self-reflection. I've unraveled mysteries, journeyed through history, and been uplifted by tales of human triumph, all from the confines of my car in traffic. And for those who cherish quiet time, fear not — there's a perfect match for you as well. Perhaps it's the soothing rhythm of a meditation podcast or the quiet unfolding of an engaging audiobook. This change turns idle moments into opportunities for enrichment.

3. My relationship with the gym is a tale of distant admiration, leading to 'deskercise' being my clandestine workout romance. It involves stealthy stretches, impromptu squats, and undercover calf raises right beneath my desk. This routine has turned into my secret for maintaining activity and giving my brain a delightful pause. The aim isn't to work up a sweat, but to disrupt the dullness of routine. Whenever

that midday lethargy creeps in, try a sky-high stretch from your chair. The sense of freedom you'll experience is surprisingly rejuvenating.

4. The Five-Senses Coffee Break: My coffee break? It's a sensory journey. It starts with watching the dark swirl of the brew, the steam rising like mist over a morning lake. I inhale the rich, earthy scent, letting it ground me before the day tries to sweep me off my feet. Each sip is savored, a small celebration of taste and warmth. The soft hum of the world around fades to a gentle lull, and for those few minutes, I'm in my bubble of calm. I'm not just drinking coffee; I'm immersing myself in a ritual that reminds me to experience life, not just live it.

5. The No-Screen Wind Down: And when night falls, I turn down the glare of screens to turn up the brightness of my inner light. Those last waking moments are mine to savor - maybe with a book that takes me worlds away or planning for a tomorrow that excites me. It's like tucking in my thoughts, ensuring they're cozy and ready for restful slumber. It's a promise to myself that the day's end is as important as its start.

So, here's to making the everyday extraordinary, to finding pockets of peace in a puzzle that's ever-shifting. These aren't just self-care rituals; they're my daily acts of defiance against a world that often forgets to pause. I encourage you to try them, tweak them, and make them yours. After all, in the rush of life, we're all just looking for a moment to catch our breath and savor the ride.

Expressive Outlets:

In the wild rapids of our everyday lives, where we're often paddling furiously just to stay afloat, the quiet moments for reflection can seem as mythical as a peaceful bathroom break when you've got kids. Believe me, I know the drill. Before the crack of dawn, we're already on duty as chauffeurs, chefs, and cheerleaders. So, let's talk about finding those small pockets of calm, those mini oases that can fit snugly into the nooks and crannies of both the bustling parent's schedule and the ever-busy individual's day. These aren't grand, time-guzzling rituals; they're more like secret handshakes with peace, brief nods to joy that we can slip into the seams of our jam-packed routines.

Let me guide you through these practices, each tailored to fit into your life, whether you're steering a solo ship or captaining a family crew. They're about making the most of the quiet eddies in the swirling stream, stitching moments of calm and joy into the fabric of your day. These practices are your lifeline to sanity in the chaos, a way to momentarily step back from the whirlwind and catch your breath. So, whether you're corralling toddlers or just corralling your thoughts, let's dive into these simple yet effective self-care rituals, and remember — in this rapid river of life, it's okay to pause and just float for a bit.

1. Multi-Tasking Morning Brew: Let's face it, mornings can either be a serene scene straight out of a meditation app or resemble a zoo during feeding time. In my routine, the pivotal element is the morning brew. Grasping that warm mug feels like taking command of the day ahead. For those enjoying solitude, each sip offers a period of introspection, a quiet internal pep talk. For parents, this time transforms into an engaging mini-forum with the kids, where the night's dreams and the day's challenges (like tackling math homework) are shared. This ritual carves out a slice of sanity, whether enjoyed in peaceful solitude or amid shared laughter, setting the

tone before plunging into the day's hustle and bustle.

2. Playlist for All Ages: Think of this as your daily score — the soundtrack that sets the stage for life's scenes, from the tranquil to the chaotic. When I'm solo, my playlist is a mixtape of mood boosters and soul soothers, shifting gears from the morning rush to the evening unwind. In the family band? It's a collaborative chart-topper, where every member gets to DJ. Picture this: cooking breakfast with Beethoven, carpool karaoke to cartoon themes, and dishwasher unloading to disco. It's not just background noise; it's the rhythm of our daily dance, keeping our spirits in sync.

3. Walk and Wonder: Whether it's pacing the pavement alone or leading a small parade of curious kiddos, walking is my secret weapon against the day's doldrums. Solo, it's my think tank on the move, where ideas breathe and problems shrink. With the family, it's an outdoor classroom – "Look, a squirrel! Why do leaves fall? Can we eat acorns?" Suddenly, a simple walk becomes a nature trail filled with wonders. It's about stepping away from screens and routines, into a world where every step is a story and every breeze a breath of fresh perspective.

4. Balanced Boundaries: Mastering the art of saying 'no' can be likened to the quest for the perfect pair of jeans – success lies in finding the right fit. In my life, saying 'no' doesn't create barriers; instead, it establishes clear boundaries. In the professional realm, it involves protecting my time to prioritize quality work over an overwhelming quantity. As a parent, it serves as a lesson for my children on the importance of

downtime. When they ask, "Can we build a rocket?" my response is affirmative, yet time-bound – "Sure, but let's do it after dinner." This practice revolves around setting and managing realistic expectations, both for others and myself. It ensures my affirmative responses carry weight and sincerity, and my declines are respectful and considered. Ultimately, a strategically placed 'no' often paves the way for a more meaningful 'yes'..

5. Evening Reflections, Family Edition: Nighttime in my house is like closing a chapter in a book. If I'm riding solo, it's a moment to jot down thoughts, a brain dump that clears the way for peaceful sleep. With my troop, it's a storytelling session where the day's lead characters share their triumphs and bloopers. It's our way of celebrating the small stuff – from acing a test to finally remembering where we left the remote. This reflection is like a nightly high-five, acknowledging our wins and learning from our stumbles, ensuring that we close the day with a sense of accomplishment and a dash of anticipation for what's to come.

Incorporating these practices into our hectic daily routines, whether we're going solo or leading a family pack, revolves around embracing brief moments of joy and serenity. This approach maximizes the inherent chaos of life, finding rhythm in the midst of frenzy, and ensuring laughter remains part of our journey. Ultimately, these small rituals become our guide through the wonderfully chaotic journey of life, making each day a little more manageable and a lot more enjoyable.

And there we have it, the end of Chapter 2, where we've dived into the art of internal tune-ups and emotional DIY. Healing from within isn't a job we can outsource; it's a hands-on project, a labor of love that's all about rolling up the sleeves of our souls and getting to work.

Now, before we flip to the next chapter, let's pause and sprinkle a little secret ingredient into the mix - laughter. That's right, as we continue our journey, I'm going to switch gears and add a dash of humor to our soul-searching adventure. Why? Because life's too short to always take the serious route, and let's be honest, a good laugh can be just as healing as a deep meditation session. So, as we dive deeper, expect a few more chuckles, some light-hearted banter, and maybe even a pun or two (no promises on the quality though).

We're going to carry forward not just the lessons and insights but also the lighter moments, the kind of laughter that bubbles up when you least expect it. Here's to embracing the healing process with a smile, to finding strength not just in struggle but also in the joy of small victories and the ridiculousness of our human foibles. Buckle up, my friends, the road to healing is not just paved with self-love, but it's also lined with laughter. The journey ahead? It's going to be enlightening, sure, but also a whole lot of fun. So, let's keep rolling – next stop: a little more heart, a little more hilarity, and a whole lot of 'How To Be Loved'."

Top of Form

Step Three

—Communicating Authentically

♥

Strap in, my friends, as we embark on a journey across the bridge of authentic communication, a path marked by my own stumbles, dances, and cartwheels. This adventure connects your heart's hushed secrets with the world's grand narrative, transforming whispers into declarations and feelings into stories that resonate. This chapter offers more than advice; it shares confessions from a fellow traveler who's navigated the rocky paths of expression and emerged with a map to guide others.

I learned the hard way that my voice wasn't just a tool for filling silence; it was a conduit for my truest self. There was a time when my words were like timid guests at a party—hovering on the edges, nodding along, seldom daring to step into the center. It was the day I decided to speak up, during a heated debate where I felt more than just passion—I felt an obligation to my own beliefs—that I truly understood the power of my voice. That moment was my rite of passage, the turning point where I went from echoing others to echoing my own soul.

It was a moment of stark miscommunication that opened my eyes. I had misinterpreted a conversation, leading to agreement in words but discomfort in feelings among those involved. This incident was a wake-up call, making me realize the true importance of listening—not just hearing words, but truly understanding their meaning and the emotions behind them.

And then there's the delicate dance of conflict, a tango I once believed was about fancy footwork to sidestep issues or outmaneuver opposition. Life handed me a different tune when I found myself in a dance of disagreement with a loved one. Instead of stepping on toes, I learned to pause, to invite their perspective, to ask with genuine curiosity, "Tell me more, so I can understand." This shift from a battle to a ballet opened my eyes to the beauty of resolving conflicts with grace and mutual respect.

So here we stand, at the threshold of a chapter that's close to my heart because it's woven from my own missteps and milestones. I'm here to share the path to a world where your voice is not just noise but a melody that sings true, where listening is not just hearing but feeling, and where conflicts are not ends but bends in the road, leading to new horizons. Let's walk this bridge together, one honest word at a time.

"Authentic communication is the bridge between your soul and the world." Alright, let's ground this thing. Communication. It's not some high-falutin' concept. It's as basic as it gets: talking and listening, as old as dirt and just as essential. Picture this: a bridge. Not the Golden Gate or anything fancy, but an old-school wooden one, creaky and a bit wobbly, that gets you from here to there. That's authentic communication. It's built from the stuff we say, the pauses we take to breathe, and the honest-to-goodness way we let our true selves show.

When you're about to have a heart-to-heart, that's you, toeing the start line of the bridge. Sure, it's a bit nerve-wracking. Will it hold? Will I make it to the other side without dropping my groceries into the river below? Here's the thing: every time you choose to speak your truth, to really listen, you're taking a step on that bridge. And I won't sugarcoat it — sometimes, it's going to sway like a hammock in a hurricane. But hang tight. Speak from the heart, listen like you mean it, and before you know it, you'll be strolling across like it's your daily walk in the park. Because, at the end of the day, crossing this bridge means connecting — really connecting — with the people around you, and that's what makes the trek worth it.

Finding Your Voice: Finding your voice can feel like rummaging through a sock drawer for a matching pair, buried under an assortment of odd ones. This quest isn't about becoming a town crier (unless you're into bell ringing and public proclamations). Instead, sift through the noise in your head to unearth what you genuinely want to say. Trust me, once you start, it's akin to hitting 'mute' on a blaring infomercial — everything becomes much clearer.

1. The Dinner Table Declaration unfolds at the family dinner table, where the casserole, comparable to bagpipes at dawn, is not exactly your cup of tea. This is your moment to step onto the stage of personal truth. Instead of the autopilot response, muster the courage to express your preference: "You know, I think I'll skip the casserole tonight. But hey, those mashed potatoes look fantastic!" It's a small step but a significant one.

By choosing honesty over obligatory politeness, you're not just sidestepping a culinary ordeal; you're establishing a space where your choices are heard and respected. This approach mirrors the candidness of a two-year-old faced with broccoli — straightforward and surprisingly effective..

2. The Meeting Room Maneuver: In the wild world of corporate meetings, it often feels like you're navigating a quirky, unpredictable sea. Imagine you're at the helm of a ship in a meeting, armed only with your PowerPoint and quick wit. When someone proposes an idea that's about as practical as a screen door on a submarine, remember to stay calm. Take a moment, then put forward your thoughts with a mix of tact and honesty: 'I've got a different angle on this.' It's not about causing a stir; it's about steering the discussion in a direction that makes sense. With every thoughtful counterpoint or alternative idea you offer, you're not just another face in the room; you're an active, guiding force. Before you know it, your meetings transform from aimless drifts to purposeful voyages towards clearer, more effective solutions.

3. The Social Media Strategy: Let's wade into the digital stream of consciousness that is social media. It's often a highlight reel, a parade of perfect moments. But it's the behind-the-scenes, the blooper reel, that people connect with. Before you add to the echo chamber with another repost, consider sharing a snippet from your own life. Maybe it's a selfie with your hair looking like you've just lost a fight with a static balloon. Or a status about how you managed to cook pasta without setting off the smoke alarm — a personal victory. It's these authentic shares that resonate more than

any filtered sunset. They say, "Hey, I'm human, and I bet you are too!"

So, as we conclude this introduction and get ready to delve deeper, keep in mind that finding your voice revolves around fully embracing your unique self. Confidently amplify your personal truths, regardless of the setting. Whether at the dinner table, in the conference room, or amidst the vast expanse of social media, your voice is the unique melody that narrates your life's story. Let it resonate loud and clear, unfettered and authentic.

Listening Deeply:

Active listening is less about lending an ear and more about opening up a whole theme park for the person speaking. You're not just sitting on a bench eating cotton candy; you're riding the rollercoaster with them, feeling every twist and turn. It's like being a DJ at the decks, syncing up to the rhythm of their words, the bass of their body language, and the melody of their tone. Now, let's break down this symphony of understanding into five digestible parts that even the busiest minds can munch on.

1. The Sherlock Holmes Scan: Prepare to listen by engaging your inner detective. This isn't just about hearing a story; it's an exercise in observation, akin to watching a live performance. Pay attention to the fluttering hands showing excitement or the furrowed brow indicating concern. These details are integral to the silent movie unfolding before your eyes. The next time a friend shares their weekend adventures, engage fully, not just with nods but with keen observation. Their animated gestures often convey more than their words.

This approach is akin to reading the subtitles in a foreign film — it adds depth and color to the story being told.

2. The Echo Technique: This is about giving their words a gentle boomerang back to them. When someone shares a piece of their day, toss it back with a twist. If they say, "My morning was a disaster," you might quip, "So, a typical Monday blockbuster, then?" It shows you're not only on their wavelength; you're adding a bit of surround sound to the experience. This technique isn't just about repetition; it's about remixing their tune with a beat of your understanding.

3. The Pause Button: Hit the brakes on the urge to jump in with your two cents. When they pause, resist the temptation to fill the void with your own symphony. Let that silence hang for a second; it's where the deeper stuff often bubbles up to the surface. Give them space to take the stage for a solo performance. It's like waiting for the popcorn to finish popping — patience brings the full bucket.

4. The Curious Cat: Curiosity is the ticket to a deeper dive into the conversation pool. When you ask questions that show genuine interest, you're not just passing the ball back and forth; you're starting a game of conversational catch that could lead anywhere. "How did that come about?" or "What did you do next?" are like opening new doors in a maze of chat, inviting them to lead you through new twists and turns.

5. The No-Judgment Zone: Approach active listening as if you are a gardener tending to their thoughts, rather than a critic ready to pounce. When someone entrusts you with

the fragile sprout of their story, handle it with care. Refrain from trampling it with judgment; instead, nurture it with understanding and respect. Allow their narrative to bloom under the nurturing sunshine of your undivided attention, eschewing the temptation to cross-examine or overanalyze their words.

And there we go, folks — active listening demystified into five friendly pointers. It's less about nodding politely while secretly planning dinner and more about diving into the conversation with a snorkel and flippers, ready to explore the depths. Keep these tips in your back pocket, and you'll be the conversation companion everyone seeks out, the one who doesn't just hear, but truly listens.

Resolving Conflict:

This one's for the time-starved, the schedule-jugglers, the folks who multitask their coffee sipping with sock matching and treat a moment's peace like a rare treasure trove. If your daily planner looks more like a tactical operation chart, and the idea of 'long talks' makes you glance nervously at your overflowing to-do list, you're in the right place. Conflict resolution? You'd prefer it express-delivered, no assembly required, because who has the time to sit around watching the drama unfold like a slow-cooker recipe?

Let's face it, for those of us who squeeze in a bathroom break between meetings and consider a five-minute coffee break the equivalent of a tropical vacation, drawn-out disagreements are about as welcome as a snowstorm in July. You want your problem-solving like your internet connection: fast, efficient, and with minimal buffering. When tension arises, you're looking for the life-hack version of peace-making —

something that could fit into a commercial break and doesn't require you to meditate on a mountaintop for seven days straight.

That's why we're cutting to the chase, giving you the quick, the witty, and the 'let's wrap this up, I've got a cake in the oven' approach to smoothing things over. Because, honestly, if you wanted to watch something dry, you'd at least choose nail polish – it's faster, and you end up with a sparkly finish. So, let's dive into conflict resolution that's faster than a microwave minute and more satisfying than peeling off that plastic film on a new phone.

1. The Curiosity Warm-Up: When something's off, like discovering your partner has given the kids ice cream for dinner (again), instead of going full-on courtroom drama, start with a curious quip. "Going for parent of the year with dessert for dinner, huh?" It's lighthearted, gets to the point, and opens up the floor for discussion without the guilt trip. Curiosity is your secret weapon; it's like the difference between a scalpel and a sledgehammer – both will make an impact, but one's a lot less messy.

2. The Gentleman's Spin: Imagine your colleague is appropriating your ideas as their own. Instead of directly accusing them of intellectual theft, you can approach the situation with a light-hearted comment: "Hey, I noticed you liked my last idea. How about we start a fan club for it?" This method is a playful yet effective way to address the issue. The approach is akin to sending a clear, direct text message rather than dispatching a carrier pigeon – it's swift, unambiguous, and avoids unnecessary complications.

3. The Synchronized Step: Encountering a teenager's grumbles about curfew calls for some fine-tuned active listening. Rather than launching into a 'back in my day' narrative, try a more engaging approach like, "Seems you're eager to party like it's 2099. Let's discuss the curfew rationale." This method demonstrates that you're really listening and empathizing with their desire for fun, yet it also underscores the importance of rules. It combines validation of their feelings with a firm reminder of boundaries, balancing understanding and structure.

4. The Dip of Understanding: Let's say you're fed up with your significant other's habit of leaving laundry everywhere. Communicate how it makes you feel without turning it into laundry Armageddon. A little humor can help: "Is the couch the new laundry basket, or are we starting a new home decor trend?" It's a nudge, not a nuclear option, like using a feather duster instead of a bulldozer to clear a little dust.

5. The Graceful Exit: After a robust discussion, look for a lighthearted way to conclude and shift gears. For instance, if doing dishes is a collective family dread, transform it into a playful challenge. Suggest something like, 'Let's try Dish Lotto! Draw a chore from the hat, and may the odds be ever in your favor.' This approach ensures a cheerful closure, guarantees everyone feels considered, and adds a dash of excitement to the resolution. It's a tactic that not only seeks fairness but also infuses a bit of fun into everyday tasks.

And there you have it—a no-nonsense guide to cutting through the daily drama without the need for a PhD in Peace Studies. Real-life scenarios? Check. A sprinkle of humor to keep things light? Double-check. Because when push comes to shove, we're all just trying to get through the day without adding 'World-Class Mediator' to our already crowded resumes. We're dealing with conflicts as they come, not with grand gestures or flowery speeches, but with the practicality of someone tightening a screw on a shaky chair leg—efficiently, without fanfare, and most importantly, without making it anyone else's problem.

Let's be honest, most of us would rather watch a three-hour documentary on the history of watching paint dry than sit through another minute of bickering about whose turn it is to take out the garbage. So we tackle these little skirmishes of life with the same gusto as plugging in a USB correctly on the first try—swiftly, smartly, and with a silent self-five when we get it right. We're not here to drag out the battles; we're here to smooth them over like we're ironing a shirt for a job interview—quick, effective, and hopefully without burning anything. Carry this toolkit with you, and you'll find that even the most unstable 'table legs' of daily life can be dealt with—a little humor, a touch of savvy, and the right-sized wrench.

Step Four – Fostering Intimacy and Trust

♥

"Trust is the fruit of a relationship in which you know you are loved."

Picture this: You're standing in the produce aisle of life, and trust is the ripe, juicy peach you're eyeing up. It's not sitting there all alone; it's nestled among bunches of love, care, and mutual respect. This peach of trust didn't just pop up out of nowhere. It grew from the roots of being loved, watered with kindness, and sprouted from the assurance that, yes, you're valued.

Why this fruity metaphor, you ask? Well, as the author, I didn't pluck it from thin air; I chose it because it's relatable. Everyone knows the satisfaction of biting into a perfect peach and the disappointment when it's all pit and no party. Similarly, trust is satisfying, nourishing, and sometimes a bit messy. It's the sweet payoff in a relationship where you've done the hard work of tending to each other's needs, and now you get to enjoy the fruits of your labor.

I liked this hook because it's simple and juicy with meaning. It resonates on a personal level because we've all been there—basking in the warm glow of being loved, feeling safe enough to let our guard down. That's when trust blooms. It's not like one of those fruits that are all show and no taste; trust is the real deal, the kind of fruit that makes the whole salad—a.k.a., the relationship—come together.

And how does this tie into Chapter 4? Well, this chapter is all about nurturing that garden where the trust-fruit grows. We'll be getting our hands dirty, dealing with the weeds of doubt and the pests of miscommunication. Because, let's be honest, nobody's relationship garden is free of them. But with a bit of humor to lighten the load and some tried-and-true techniques, we'll get to the root of how to cultivate that trust-fruit until it's ripe for the picking.

So there you have it. Trust as a fruit is not just a throwaway line; it's a whole philosophy packed into a pit... I mean, nutshell. It's the tasty teaser for a chapter that promises to be as refreshing as a fruit salad on a hot day—filling, full of variety, and just a little bit sweet.

Building trust is a bit like assembling flat-pack furniture: it should be straightforward, but sometimes you need a little patience, a few tools, and the ability to not throw the instruction manual – or your relationship – out the window.

Let's start with the basics. Trust is built on the small stuff. Take the time I told my partner I'd sort the laundry. It wasn't a declaration of love; it was a promise to separate whites from colors. But when I actually delivered on that promise, it was like I'd handed over a bouquet of freshly ironed shirts. It's actions, not just sweet nothings whispered at midnight, that build trust.

Now, trust also encompasses sharing those less-than-spotless moments. Like confessing to your roommate that you were the culprit behind the mysterious disappearance of the last pizza slice, not a phantom snack burglar. This kind of honesty is akin to the transparency of a cartoon glass door, even when it means you're the center of the jest. It's a step towards fostering a deeper connection through vulnerability and a good-humored admission of your own imperfections.

And when life throws a wrench in the works, like the time I scratched my sister's car, trust means fessing up before she turned into an amateur detective. Sure, it would've been easier to let her blame the neighbor's cat, but honesty won out. It wasn't just her car that got dinged, but potentially my credibility, too.

Then there's navigating the minefield of boundaries. Imagine a coworker keeps calling you after hours to "quickly" chat about work. Setting a boundary can be as simple as saying, "Hey, after 6 PM, my phone turns into a pumpkin, and so does my brain." It's a light-hearted way to reinforce that your time off is non-negotiable, kind of like that gym membership you optimistically signed up for.

Wrapping it all up, trust isn't an elusive, high-brow concept. It's the fundamental meat and potatoes of relationships, akin to the daily bread that nourishes them. Picture trust as reliable as your favorite pair of well-worn jeans and as authentic as the expression you make when you unexpectedly catch your reflection in the front camera.

Consistently nurturing this kind of trust builds a foundation strong enough to withstand even the most chaotic flat-pack furniture assembly disasters.

Building Trust:

Think of trust as the good old Wi-Fi of your relationship. It's got to be strong, or you'll be watching the spinning wheel of death on the loading screen of your relationship drama. Now, let's break down this trust-building business into five easy-peasy, lemon-squeezy steps.

1. Honesty: Say It Like It Is Honesty is your relationship's tech support. It troubleshoots the little hiccups before they become full-blown connectivity issues. Let's say you accidentally backed into your partner's car. Instead of concocting an elaborate story about a rogue shopping cart, be upfront. Admit it was you, your foot, and a tragic misjudgment of reverse gear. It might sting at the moment, but it prevents that 'I-can't-believe-you-lied' virus from infecting your trust. Honesty shows you're not just about talk; you're about truth, even when it's about admitting that, yes, you did eat the last cookie and blamed it on the dog.

2. Consistency: Be the Human Calendar Now onto consistency, the unsung hero of trust. It's like those reliable old appliances that just keep chugging along. If you say you're going to do something, do it. Whether it's taking out the trash or calling them right back, be as predictable as those infomercials that promise you a revolutionary kitchen gadget for three easy payments of $19.99. When you follow through time and time again, you become the human equivalent of a

calendar alert – dependable, expected, and always on time.

3. Communication: The Open Book Strategy. Imagine communication as having full cell phone bars — clear, uninterrupted, and direct. It's like ensuring there's no static, no frustrating 'Can you hear me now?' moments. Instead of offering just a summary on the back cover of your life's book, you're inviting someone to read the chapter you're currently living. For instance, if work's been hectic, leaving you more frazzled than a balloon at a static electricity convention, share those details. Explain the reasons behind your late-night typing marathons or your distant gaze during dinner. This level of sharing fosters understanding and deepens connections.

4. Listening: Tune In, Really In Listening goes beyond simply waiting for your turn to speak. It involves genuinely tuning into the frequency of their broadcast. When someone shares their day with you, it's not a cue for you to mentally compile your grocery list. Instead, listen as if you're preparing for a quiz on their words, complete with multiple-choice questions about the details. If they express worries about a new colleague taking credit for their ideas, resist the urge to counter with your own work saga. Instead, offer an empathetic nod, showing you truly understand, and encourage them to share more with a supportive 'That sucks. Tell me more."

5. Action: Walk the Talk Finally, we've got action – the boots on the ground of building trust. Actions speak louder than a megaphone at a library. If you promise breakfast in bed, deliver that tray complete with their favorite waffles and a

decent cup of coffee. Don't just offer a raincheck because you hit snooze one too many times. When they see you putting words into action, it's like watching their favorite book come to life – thrilling, satisfying, and it makes them eager for the next chapter.

Wrap all this up, and you've got a trust-building strategy that's as straightforward as a toddler's logic and as relatable as finding that mysterious Tupperware at the back of the fridge. Be your authentic self, show up consistently, and become the MVP of their support system. Adopt these practices, and you'll establish trust as robust as the Wi-Fi in a teenager's bedroom.

Deepening Connection:

Building intimacy and trust doesn't require you to scale a cliff face or sit cross-legged atop a mountain, unless, of course, that's your ideal date scenario. It's actually much simpler and can be done in your very own living room. It's the small actions that pack a punch, the kind that don't scream "I love you" from the rooftops but whisper it in the grocery store aisle when you pass them the chocolate they love without them having to ask.

It's in the way you remember how they take their coffee and have it ready before they've even stumbled out of bed, blurry-eyed and grumbling about the alarm. It's in the knowing glance you share when "that" friend starts detailing their exotic vacation for the umpteenth time, and you both have to stifle your giggles. It's this shared language, developed in the trenches of daily life, that fortifies your bond. Trust is built into these micro-moments, like when they're late coming home and instead of a barrage of texts asking "Where are you?" you send one that simply says, "Everything cool?" It's a vote of confidence, a statement of faith, and a small deposit into your mutual trust fund.

And understanding? It comes from really seeing them. Not just noticing that they're wearing their favorite shirt (the one you've secretly come to despise), but recognizing the slight slump of their shoulders after a hard day. It's about picking up on the hesitation in their voice when they say they're fine, and you know they're anything but. That's your cue to pull out your best jokes or simply sit beside them in silence, offering the comfort of your presence. That's how you build a fortress of trust and intimacy – not with grand gestures or epic promises, but with a consistent, reliable presence and the kind of understanding that needs no words, just a shared smile over the perfectly timed delivery of a punchline that no one else gets.

1. Inside Jokes: Your Secret Handshake Inside jokes really are the secret handshakes of any solid relationship. They're the kind of jokes that would make zero sense to a bystander but have you and your partner in stitches every time. Like that time you both saw a dog so fluffy it looked like a moving bathmat, and now every shaggy dog you see is "Bathmat Brian." These shared giggles create a private comedy club where the two of you are always the headliners. Each time you reference that one time you both mistook an elderly man for a department store mannequin, it's like an inside high-five. It's not just laughter; it's an echo of a shared history that only you two can hear.

But it's not just about rehashing old laughs; it's about creating new ones that join the pantheon of your personal jokes. Maybe it's the way you pronounce 'spaghetti' as 'pasketti' just because it once made your partner snort tea out of their nose. It's a reminder that you both find the same things oddly hilarious, and in a world that can be too serious, that's a golden nugget. Next time you're both in a tense situation, like sitting in a too-quiet waiting room, just a subtle whisper of "Bathmat Brian" can be a silent symphony of hilarity just for two, turning a mundane moment into an inside joke factory.

2. Non-Verbal Nudges: Beyond Words Then there's the art of non-verbal communication, the kind of intuitive understanding that can feel almost telepathic. Your partner doesn't need to say a word; their sigh as they drop onto the couch is as loud as a foghorn for "I've had a day." And your response with a mug of their favorite coffee and their comfy slippers is the equivalent of saying "I hear you" louder than any words could. It's like an invisible dance you both have perfected over time, where every shrug, eye roll, or deep breath communicates volumes.

This silent language can transform mundane moments into meaningful exchanges. When you're at a party and your partner is trapped in a never-ending conversation, just a quick glance and subtle head tilt towards the door can be your joint escape plan. It's like being spies at a social gathering, where a raised eyebrow is the signal for "It's time to go." And when they do the secret 'I'm bored' signal, you swoop in with a fake urgent call to rescue them. It's teamwork at its finest, no decoder ring needed.

3. Hug it Out: The Stress-Buster Grip Hugs, the universal language of "I've got you," are the ultimate stress busters. When your partner comes through the door, face longer than a CVS receipt, engulf them in a hug that's like a human stress ball. It's not a hug of mere formality, like shaking hands with a distant relative; it's a hug that envelops them, a physical manifestation of "we're in this together." It's the sort that

pauses time, squeezes out the worry, and sometimes even lifts you off your feet.

And it's not just for the bad days. Celebratory hugs can be just as impactful. Your partner got a promotion? Pick them up and spin them around in a hug that's part circus act, part pure joy. It's these moments that fortify the connection between you, turning a simple embrace into a fortress of comfort and solidarity. It's a reminder that no matter what the world throws at you, in the sanctuary of each other's arms, you're home.

4. Chore Wars: The Stealth Operation Acts of service are the ninjas of love languages. They sneak up on you with their quiet support and can often be more romantic than a dozen roses. It's doing the dishes when it's not your turn, or taking the car for an oil change because you know they hate doing it. These are the unsung hero moments that say "I love you" in a dialect of diligence. It's like silently replacing the toilet roll—it might go unnoticed, but it speaks volumes.

But these acts of service also come with their share of humor. Like when you pretend to be the 'Laundry Whisperer,' speaking to the clothes as if they'll fold themselves if you coax them gently enough. Or when you 'accidentally' make their favorite cookies when you know they've had a bad day. It's a covert operation where the mission is simple: make their day a little brighter, a little lighter, and a whole lot cleaner.

5. Quality Time: Quality time means creating a no-phone zone, an oasis in the digital desert where screens are banished, and attention is king. Commit to being fully present, whether you're engaging in playful debates about culinary conundrums or trying to assemble

furniture without instructions. Give each other the gift of undivided attention, a rarity in the age of constant digital noise.

In these moments, cooking together turns the kitchen into a laboratory for laughter and culinary mishaps. Quiet evenings under a blanket become special, with warmth stemming from shared comfort and silence as cozy as an old t-shirt. It's understanding that time spent together, just the two of you, outshines any blockbuster movie or social event. It's the treasure of uninterrupted time, more coveted than the last slice of pizza you both secretly yearn for.

Maintain a light-hearted approach, infuse these moments with meaning, and allow your genuine selves to come forth. These are the times that forge an unbreakable bond, one that can find humor in life's misadventures and still savor the joy of togetherness

These moments, shared in the kitchen, transform cooking into an adventure filled with laughter and culinary escapades. Similarly, quiet evenings under a blanket become cherished times, with warmth coming not only from the wool but also from the comfort of shared silence as familiar and cozy as an old t-shirt. Being together, just the two of you, surpasses the allure of any blockbuster movie or bustling social event. The uninterrupted time you spend together becomes a luxury, more valuable than the last coveted slice of pizza, which both of you claim to not want but secretly desire.

Keep it light, keep it meaningful, and let the real, unedited version of yourselves shine. These moments are the ones that build an indestructible bond, the kind that can laugh in the face of life's burnt casseroles and still enjoy the feast of being together.

Honoring Boundaries: Bottom of Form Setting boundaries is all about striking that delicate balance between togetherness and individuality. It's not that you're anti-fun; you're just pro-sanity. Think of it as the difference between an open-door policy and keeping the door ajar—you're welcoming but not to the point where your life resembles a 24/7 convenience store. It's about communicating clearly that while you adore your significant other's adventurous spirit, you also cherish peace and quiet. It's setting up the relational Wi-Fi to power down at a reasonable hour, so everyone gets the rest they need. And just like with Wi-Fi, sometimes you need that password-protected space to ensure your personal bandwidth isn't stretched to the breaking point. In practice, this means sitting down together and figuring out where you both need a little breathing room. It's like deciding which apps get to run in the background of your phone; some you need on all the time, like messages from your partner, and others can be put on sleep mode, like work emails after hours. It's a mutual agreement that ensures when you're together, you're really there, fully charged and present, not just a shell running on low battery because your boundaries were too porous.

Finally, it's important to remember that boundaries aren't about keeping someone out; they're about creating a healthy space for your relationship to flourish. It's the equivalent of having a cozy room where you can retreat and recharge, rather than a bustling train station where anyone and anything can come barreling through at any moment. Setting these limits is less about saying "keep out" and more about saying "this is my space, and I'll invite you in when I'm ready." It's a way to preserve the integrity of your personal and shared lives, ensuring that both get the respect and attention they deserve.

1. The 'We Need to Talk' Talk Starting the boundary conversation is as popular as scheduling a root canal, but it's got to be done. Imagin you are sitting down and laying out your soul like you're folding laundry in front of an audience. "Listen," you say, trying to keep the nervous laughter at bay, "I treasure our midnight philosophical debates about whether pets know we're petting them or if they just think we're swatting flies, but I need to catch the train to dreamland before midnight." It's all about being honest without making them feel like they're being handed a cease-and-desist letter for being themselves.

This talk shouldn't feel like a business meeting, though. Keep it casual, maybe over a shared pizza, where you can slide in a "By the way..." between bites. It's finding the balance between "I need to sleep" and "I love hearing about your alien conspiracy theories." And remember, timing is key. Don't drop the boundary bomb just as they're gushing about their day. Wait for the lull, when the only sound is the distant bark of that dog that might be a little too obsessed with the moon.

After the talk, it's like a weight has been lifted. Suddenly, your evenings have a curfew that isn't enforced by a grumpy landlord, but by mutual respect. And as you both stick to this newfound pact, the under-eye bags begin to retreat, and the mornings feel less like a zombie apocalypse and more like an actual new beginning.

2. The 'No, Thanks' Exercise involves mastering the delicate balance between your needs and your partner's. For instance, when the idea of hosting another one of your partner's work parties feels overwhelming, it's perfectly okay to choose tranquility over social obligations. Suggest an alternative that suits both of you, like proposing, "Love, how about we turn this fiesta into a siesta?" This approach allows you to assert your preferences without diminishing theirs.

Consider it akin to navigating a challenging yoga pose; you need to find flexibility without compromising your well-being. If your partner plans a weekend brimming with activities that seem exhausting, you can suggest a middle ground. For example, propose, "How about we explore that new hiking trail on Saturday and reserve Sunday for some relaxing downtime?" This kind of negotiation isn't about rejecting their ideas outright; rather, it's finding a mutual sweet spot where both of your needs are met.

And when you get this step right, it's liberating. Suddenly, the calendar isn't a tyrant, and you're not playing tag with burnout. Instead, you're finding joy in the things you do say yes to, and there's no resentment brewing like a forgotten teabag that's steeped too long.

3. The Mutual Respect Pact Respecting each other's boundaries is a fundamental act of love and respect, similar to understanding and accepting their needs without intrusion. If your partner requires time alone to unwind after work, give them that space. It's not a reflection of their feelings towards you; it's simply their way of transitioning from work mode to home life.

It's all about understanding. When they flop down with that 'do not disturb' vibe, give them space. And in return, they'll learn to recognize when you need a sounding board for your latest "Why is life like this?" monologue. It's give and take, a dance of knowing when to step forward and when to step back.

But this mutual respect thing? It's as sweet as it gets. When it works, your relationship becomes a well-oiled machine, humming along, with each part functioning just right. You're in sync, and the gears of daily life grind a little less and glide a bit more. It's not about keeping score; it's focused on maintaining peace.

4. The Check-In Boundaries may be more like your favorite pair of stretchy pants than a pair of stiff jeans. They've got to have some give. Regular check-ins are where you reassess and recalibrate. It's sitting down over coffee and saying, "So, about our horror flick Fridays—I've been having nightmares about being chased by a killer tomato. Can we switch to rom-coms?"

This step is about staying flexible and keeping the communication lines as open as the 24-hour diner down the street. Life changes, needs shift, and the boundaries that worked last month might be chafing now. The check-in is like a system update for your relationship software; it keeps things running smoothly and glitch-free.

Celebrate the wins when these check-ins help. Maybe you've successfully swapped out movie night for a puzzle challenge, and now the evenings are filled with more "Aha!" moments than "Ahh!" screams. It's proof that with a little tweaking, the rhythm of your relationship can evolve into a melody that suits both of your tastes.

5. The Celebration of Space Finally, celebrating the space that boundaries provide is like throwing a party because you finally cleaned out that closet you've been afraid to open for months. It's taking a Saturday for yourself, doing whatever it is that recharges your batteries, and not feeling a lick of guilt about it. It's understanding that loving each other doesn't mean you have to be joined at the hip; it means loving each other enough to enjoy your separate hobbies, friends, and yes, even TV shows.

This celebration involves basking in togetherness when you're, well, together, and savoring solitude when you're apart. It's like having two flavors of ice cream in the freezer; you don't always need to share the same scoop. The beauty lies in reuniting after a day apart, brimming with new stories and fresh energy to invest in each other.

When you nail this, your relationship feels like a well-designed home. There's a room for every mood, a space for every need, and a common area where memories are made. In this balanced dance of life, you and your partner twirl together, careful not to step on each other's toes. It's ensuring the right distance and closeness, not creating separation but cherishing the togetherness it brings.

Honoring boundaries resembles being a DJ at a silent disco, where you're attuned to different wavelengths to keep everyone in sync. It's not about strict rules or sternly wagging a finger every time personal space is encroached. It's more about subtly suggesting the joy of having one's own portion of something, like those irresistible fries. After all, love might involve sharing a life, but that doesn't necessarily extend to sharing every last thing. It's giving each other adequate space on life's dance floor, ensuring both can bust their moves, like the funky chicken, without causing a ruckus.

When you've got the boundary-setting down, your relationship starts to feel less like a cramped elevator ride and more like a spacious ballroom. You're not stepping on toes or elbowing each other in the ribs; you're gliding and twirling in a rhythm that would make the stars envious. It's about knowing when to come together for the dip and when to give your partner the spotlight for their solo. Because even in a duet, a little solo shimmy can make the heart grow fonder.

But let's be real, sometimes setting boundaries feels as unnatural as eating pizza with a fork and knife. You might worry it'll put a dampener on things, like saying "no" to an extra scoop of ice cream. But in truth, it's more like choosing the right toppings everyone gets their perfect flavor. And sure, at first, you might miss those late-night ice cream binges until you realize that not waking up feeling like you've swallowed a bowling ball is kind of nice.

So, when you and your partner start respecting each other's need for space, whether it's an hour of uninterrupted bath time or a sacred Sunday morning lie-in, you're not building walls; you're laying down the welcome mat on your terms. It's like creating a home with rooms tailored to each of your needs, complete with a cozy joint living area where the two of you can come together and share the highlights of your day. That's the dance of boundaries – it's choreographed to the beat of mutual respect, personal freedom, and the kind of love that knows when to hold on tight and when to let go just enough.

As we close the curtains on Chapter 4, let's take a moment to reflect on the journey we've embarked on. We've navigated the winding roads of trust and intimacy, learning that these aren't just lofty ideals found in fairy tales, but real, tangible elements that make or break the everyday magic of relationships. We've laughed, nodded in agreement, and maybe even had a few "aha" moments along the way. It's been a bit like going through an old photo album, where each picture tells a story of connection, misunderstanding, and learning to dance in the rain of life's challenges.

Now, standing at the gateway of Chapter 5, we have a clearer grasp on fostering trust and intimacy. We've learned that grand gestures and dramatic declarations aren't the keystones of a strong bond. Instead, the foundation lies in small, consistent acts of understanding, respect, and genuine care. We're becoming adept at interpreting our partner's unspoken language, valuing their need for personal space, and delighting in the unique rhythm of our relationship. Armed with these insights, we're poised to build stronger, more resilient connections that can withstand any challenge.

But our journey isn't over yet. In fact, it's just getting started. As we step into the next chapter, we'll dive deeper into the complexities of relationships. We'll explore how to navigate conflicts, communicate effectively, and keep the flame of passion alive over time. We'll tackle the common pitfalls that couples face and learn how to turn challenges into opportunities for growth. Think of it as advancing to the next level in the game of love, armed with new tools and insights.

So, take a deep breath and pat yourself on the back. You've come a long way, but the road ahead is exciting. As we embark on the next chapter, remember that every relationship is a journey, not a destination. There will be bumps along the way, but with humor, understanding, and a willingness to learn, there's no obstacle too big to overcome. Chapter 5 awaits, and with it, a new set of adventures in the ever-evolving landscape of love and companionship. Let's turn the page together and see what new discoveries await.

Chapter 5: Step Five – Embracing Shared Growth

"Love is not just about two people looking at each other, but looking in the same direction together."

Love is often likened to a two-way street, a shared journey, a tandem bike ride where both parties pedal in sync towards the same horizon. This journey goes beyond the knee-weakening gazes across candlelit tables, embracing the times both of you strap on your helmets, focus on mutual goals, and pedal in harmony—even through life's inevitable potholes.

As we embark on Chapter 5, we arrive at the pivotal 'Growing Together Without Growing Sick of Each Other' juncture. Here, love goes beyond the honeymoon phase of shared desserts and intertwining footsteps on the beach, evolving into a shared game plan. Now, you're engaging in more than just passing the ketchup across the diner booth; you're sketching out dreams on the back of napkins. This stage centers on the collective excitement of plotting life's next big adventure, from mastering competitive charades to budgeting for the backyard oasis you both envision.

This shared vision is the glue that binds you, stronger than any whispered sweet nothing. It's the late-night strategy sessions where you both pore over brochures for that pool, debating the merits of a slide versus a diving board. It's the high-fives when you win at game night, not just because of the victory, but because you played your cards in a rhythmic dance of mutual understanding and strategy. It's the weekends spent practicing your charade signals until you can guess 'Jurassic Park' from a simple hand gesture.

But let's dive deeper—beyond the charades and pool plans. This togetherness in vision also extends to supporting each other through both the mundane and the seismic shifts of life. It involves aligning your career goals, ensuring that one's ambition complements rather than silences the other's. This stage is about striking a balance between personal space and shared square footage, where individual growth is celebrated as an integral part of the collective bloom..

And as you look in the same direction together, you'll find that the journey is peppered with laughter, the occasional (but inevitable) misstep, and a bounty of shared experiences that become the stories you'll recount with fondness. It's in these chapters that the narrative of your relationship is written, in the ink of shared dreams and the font of mutual respect. Together, you're not just crafting a love story; you're authoring an epic tale of companionship where every chapter sings with the melody of joint aspirations.

Supporting Mutual Goals:

Alright, folks, lean in close because I'm going to let you in on a little secret of how my partner and I manage to keep our dreams in lockstep, even when our schedules are as packed as a clown car at the circus. I know what you're thinking: between work, the gym, maybe kids, and that pile of laundry that's starting to resemble a small mountain range, who's got the time? Well, believe me, I've been there, trying to balance the spinning plates of daily life on just one finger, and let me tell you, it's not just possible; it's doable without losing your marbles.

So, here's the lowdown on how we do the dream tango without stepping on each other's toes. It all starts with a commitment to not let our ambitions become ghosts that haunt the nooks and crannies of our too-busy lives. We make our couple goals a priority, not by adding more hours to the day (if only, right?), but by getting smart with the time we have. We weave our aspirations through the fabric of our daily hustle, turning 'no time' into 'go time.' It's about making every moment count, from sharing our wildest hopes over morning coffee to those whispered plans before sleep claims us.

And trust me, I understand the struggle. With a to-do list that's never-ending and a calendar that's bursting at the seams, finding time for 'us' goals can feel like trying to squeeze into your high school jeans—hopeful, but unrealistic. But with a little bit of ingenuity and a dash of dedication, we've turned our shared dreams from a 'someday' into a 'today.' Celebrating the small wins is key, like when we both manage to squeeze in a workout, or when we finally decide on the color of the kitchen—after only three debates and a near-miss with paint samples. The focus here is not on grand gestures; it's on the daily grind towards greatness, together.

1. The Power-Hour Planning Sesh First up, we've got the Power-Hour Planning Sesh. Once a week, my partner and I grab our calendars and a timer, hunker down with coffee, and go full-throttle on planning our dream-chasing for exactly one hour. No more, no less. We break down our big dreams into little action steps, like "Run for 10 minutes without looking like a winded walrus" or "Save X amount of cash by skipping that third latte." It's all about bite-sized chunks that even our crazy schedules can handle.

In those 60 minutes, we're a dynamic duo. We've got sticky notes for milestones, a whiteboard for brainstorming, and a no-phones-allowed rule. By the time the buzzer buzzes, we've got a clear game plan for the week. It's like meal-prepping, but for our goals. And let me tell you, there's nothing like the high of ticking off those tiny tasks that are marching us toward the finish line, one small victory at a time.

2. Synced-Up Sweat Sessions For our fitness dreams, we've embraced the concept of Synced-Up Sweat Sessions. We don't always exercise side by side — honestly, our workout styles are hilariously different. While I'm doing my routine, my partner's exercises can be pretty

amusing in their unique way. But what we do is align our workout schedules. We may be in separate spaces, but knowing we're both exercising at the same time brings a sense of shared effort and quirky togetherness.

We've got these apps on our phones that cheer us on and let the other know when we've wrapped up. Sometimes, it's just a simple message like, "Survived the treadmill, your turn!" It's not about the six-packs (although, not opposed), it's about sharing the journey of getting fitter, or at least less likely to pant when climbing stairs.

3. Joint Account Jive Now, onto the money moves with the Joint Account Jive. We funnel a little bit of cash into a shared savings account for those big dreams, like that mythical vacation we've been talking about since we saw it in a magazine at the dentist's office. Even if it's just the spare change from not indulging in daily designer coffees, it adds up.

Every month, we check in on our growing treasure pot. Seeing those numbers climb is like watching your favorite team score—it's a communal rush. And because it's joint, it feels like we're both contributing to this future fund of fun. No lottery needed, just good ol' fashioned saving with a dash of high-fiving each time we deposit.

4. Personal Pep-Talks Personal goals? We've got those covered with Personal Pep-Talks. We set aside time each week to coach each other on our individual ambitions. I might not know the first thing about my partner's passion for urban gardening, but I'm there with a watering can of encouragement.

We've set up little corners in our home for our personal projects. When I see my partner with dirt under their nails and a smile on their face, I know they're in their element. And when they see me with my headphones on, lost in a language learning app, they get it. We don't have to be in the same book, let alone on the same page, to cheer each other on.

5. The Monthly Recap Rendezvous Last but not least, the Monthly Recap Rendezvous. It's our monthly meeting where we look back at the steps we've taken towards our goals. We've got a corkboard where we pin pictures, notes, and anything that symbolizes progress. It's like a victory lap in our living room.

Sometimes it's celebrating that we ran a little longer, saved a little more, or just managed to keep our plants alive. Acknowledging the effort, regardless of the outcome, is crucial. During this recap, we remind each other of the importance of the journey, not just the destination. Plus, it usually involves some sort of treat, because let's face it, rewards are fantastic motivators.

So, my fellow comrades in the chronically crunched-for-time brigade, that's the skinny on syncing up with your significant other to chase those dreams without the drama. These five strategies aren't just about ticking boxes; they're about creating moments that matter, about weaving a tapestry of teamwork that's as colorful as it is strong. They're the things you'll look back on, the stories you'll tell when someone asks, "How do you do it?" And you'll smile, thinking of the chaos, the coffee, and the shared Google calendars, and say, "We just do."

But don't hang up your hats just yet, because the journey doesn't end here. Oh no, we're merely getting started. As we gear up for the next chapter, it's time to shine a spotlight on you. Yes, YOU, the individual. Because while having a partner in crime, a co-pilot in this adventure of life is fantastic, nurturing your own growth, tending to your personal garden of aspirations, and letting it flourish is just as crucial. Encouraging personal development is about giving yourself the same level of care and attention that you pour into your shared goals. It's about honoring your needs, your desires, and the things that make your soul sing with the ferocity of a private concert just for one.

So, as we turn this page and prepare to dive into the world of personal development, remember that this is your time to shine. Finding balance is key, ensuring that your own dreams bask in the sun while contributing to the beautiful duet that is your partnership. Get ready to explore the paths that lead to your personal Everest. Learn to cheer for yourself with the same enthusiasm you reserve for your shared victories. Together, we'll uncover the secrets to growing individually and how that, in turn, can make your shared journey even richer. Strap in; it's going to be an exhilarating ride.

Encouraging Personal Development:

Alright, lone wolves and dynamic duos, gather around. It's time to talk about giving your personal growth some serious legroom, even if your life's so crammed you can't swing a cat without hitting your to-do list. Whether you're flying solo or navigating the skies with a co-pilot, the '7 Simple Steps' method is your ticket to soaring high on your own terms. I'm living proof that you can spin your own yarn of success, whether you're knitting a solo scarf or a two-person quilt. So, let's unfold the map of self-improvement that caters to everyone's itinerary.

1. The Cheer-on-the-Go: Whether flying solo as your own cheerleader or having a partner chanting your name, the Cheer-on-the-Go celebrates those micro-victories. Give yourself a wink in the mirror after

nailing a presentation, or share a virtual high-five when conquering the weekly grocery shopping. Self-text a pep talk or leave an encouraging note on the fridge. These small acknowledgments of daily wins don't require a partner, but if you have one, they're your ultimate hype squad. It fits seamlessly into any lifestyle, offering a nod of recognition for all the epic things you do. Go ahead, send that congratulatory emoji to yourself or your partner, because every step forward merits its own mini-celebration..

Solo or paired up, this technique fits neatly into the busiest of lifestyles. It's the little nod of recognition that says, "Hey, I see you and all the epic stuff you're doing." So, send that congratulatory emoji to yourself or your partner because every step forward deserves its own mini parade.

2. The Synced Hobby Hour: Ideal for both singles and couples, the Synced Hobby Hour is about setting aside dedicated time for passions. Solo adventurers, treat this time as sacred; switch off distractions and dive into what ignites your spirit. For couples, it's respecting each other's 'me time.' Maybe they're strumming a guitar while you master the art of sourdough in the kitchen. This practice is less about being together and more about supporting individual growth. By valuing this uninterrupted hobby hour, you're building a personal fortress of fulfillment.

3. The Interest Q&A: This weekly practice is a date with curiosity. Singles, reflect on your week, asking, "What new thing did I learn?" It's a celebration of your curiosity and capacity for learning. For couples, it's a time to connect over new discoveries and share those unique tidbits that define you. The focus here isn't on impressing each other but on fueling the flame of curiosity that burns within us all.

4. The Mini Milestone Fiesta: Celebrating the small stuff is crucial, whether you're toasting to your own tenacity or clinking glasses with your significant other. Finished a difficult book? Pat yourself on the back with your favorite treat. Your partner finally beat that tricky level on their video game? Whip up a victory snack and join in the mini fiesta.

This practice is about transforming achievements into a festival of joy. It's a reminder that personal progress, no matter how trivial it seems, is a cornerstone of happiness. So, pop that confetti cannon for yourself, or for both of you, because every step deserves its own spotlight.

5. The Back-Yourself Badge: The Back-Yourself Badge centers on self-recognition. Look in the mirror and affirm, 'You did good, kid.' If you're single, embrace being your own biggest fan, because if you don't applaud your own show, who will? In a relationship, it means giving each other permission to bask in the glow of individual accomplishments. This silent nod of approval is the affirmation we all need from time to time.

When you back yourself, you build a reservoir of confidence that's both deeply personal and universally relatable. Whether you share that with someone else or it's just for you, the result is the same: a stronger, more resilient you, ready to take on the world.

The quest for personal growth, my dear readers, is not a solemn march to the beat of a drum. Instead, envision it as a funky, solo dance-off in your living room or a spontaneous duet in the kitchen. This chapter is a celebration of self-discovery and mutual encouragement, whether you're going solo or dancing a tango for two. For the lone wolves, it means transforming your inner whispers into a one-person rock band. For couples, it's harmonizing your life songs, carefully avoiding stepping on each other's toes. Whether single or in a relationship, growth is your background music – a mix of jazz and rock, always uniquely yours. The focus isn't on reaching a finale but on enjoying the journey, whether you're riffing a solo or jamming with a partner.

So, as we flip to the next page of our saga, let's do it with the excitement of a cliffhanger episode. The chapters ahead are more than just a narrative; they're an invitation to a life lived in high definition, with every day an opportunity for growth. Whether you're chuckling over your bloopers or high-fiving your successes, each moment is a patch in the quilt of your epic tale. To the singles: enjoy the freedom of scripting your own adventure. To those in partnerships: savor the joint venture of writing your shared story. And the plot twists? They're not hurdles; they're the hidden tracks in your life's album, waiting to be discovered. Let's welcome them with a grin and a ready spirit. Keep flipping those pages—your story's got plenty of chapters left to write.

Navigating Life Changes Together:

Hey there, you intrepid life navigators, sailing the seas of the unexpected. Whether you're flying solo or navigating the tides with your partner-in-crime, life has a knack for throwing curveballs that would make a major league pitcher green with envy. I've been through the wringer a few times myself—my life sometimes feels like a game of dodgeball where the balls are on fire and I'm blindfolded. But guess what? I've gotten pretty good at dodging, ducking, and occasionally, making a spectacular catch. So, whether you're embracing the single life with the enthusiasm of a kid in a candy store or you're part of a duo that's more dynamic than a superhero team, I've got some strategies to share. They're simple, they're effective, and they'll have you chuckling in the face of adversity.

Imagine life as a pinball machine—you're the ball being batted around by flippers, bumpers, and those pesky obstacles that seem to come out of nowhere. Sometimes, it feels like you're just bouncing from one challenge to another, racking up points in the game of life. But here's the thing: whether you're playing solo or you've got someone mashing the buttons alongside you, you've got the skills to navigate this arcade. The strategies I'm going to share aren't just about surviving; they're about thriving. They're the power-ups and cheat codes that can turn a potentially frustrating game into a high-scoring adventure.

Now, let's get down to the nitty-gritty. These five strategies are my tried-and-true methods, honed in the fires of "Well, that didn't go as planned." They're the equivalent of finding the secret passage in a maze or unlocking the bonus round where everything suddenly goes your way. And the best part? They work whether you're a lone wolf or a part of a dynamic duo. It's like having a Swiss Army knife in your pocket for life's unexpected moments. We're talking about real, practical tips that you can use in the daily grind, when the unexpected comes knocking at your door.

So, buckle up, and let's dive in. I'm about to take you on a guided tour through my playbook for handling life's curveballs with a dash of humor, a pinch of grace, and a whole lot of 'bring it on' attitude. Whether you find yourself facing a sudden downpour of challenges or just a drizzle of minor annoyances, these strategies are your umbrella—and sometimes your life raft. We'll navigate these waters together, laughing in the rain and sometimes dancing in the puddles. Because when life throws curveballs, we throw back a curve of our own—a smile. Let's turn the page and embark on this journey, ready to tackle whatever comes our way with a wink and a nod. Here we go!

1. The Quick-Draw Plan B The Quick-Draw Plan B is your trusty sidekick in the unpredictable wild west of life. Picture planning a romantic outdoor picnic and then facing an unexpected thunderstorm. Instead of a sun-kissed afternoon, you're now looking at gloomy skies. But with Plan B, you transform it into an indoor picnic, creating a cozy haven with a blanket fort and fairy lights. This move flips the script with a flourish, turning a potential washout into a charming indoor adventure.

Whether you're flying solo or part of a dynamic duo, the Quick-Draw Plan B ensures you're never at the mercy of life's caprices. It's like having a secret escape hatch when the main stage of life gets too hectic. For example, when my freelance work hit a snag, I activated Plan B by diversifying my skills – enter underwater basket weaving! For couples, it's those impromptu decisions that inject excitement into the relationship. Think of spontaneous road trips replacing disrupted weekend plans, or transforming a power outage into an intimate candlelit storytelling session.

Mastering the Quick-Draw Plan B involves agility, creativity, and a touch of audacity. It involves swiftly rewriting your script, turning each unexpected twist to your advantage. Whether you're navigating life alone or with your partner in adventure, this approach turns you into a virtuoso of adaptation, orchestrating a symphony of endless possibilities

2. The Stress-Deflector Shield The Stress-Deflector Shield is your personal armor against the myriad stressors of life. Envision yourself as

a superhero, cape in the wind, resiliently facing down every stressor like so many specks of kryptonite. When you're on your own, this might mean letting loose to your favorite tracks, dancing away the day's tensions. In a partnership, it becomes a shared task – maybe channeling stress into a creative DIY project that turns frustration into something tangible and rewarding.

Your shield is more than just a barrier against stress; it's a tool for turning it to your advantage. Personally, I've learned to find humor in chaotic moments – like when a burnt dinner becomes an excuse for an unexpected takeout adventure. For couples this principle translates to embracing the mishaps with a smile, like that hilarious kitchen fiasco when you both tried to bake a soufflé and ended up with a scene straight out of a comedy show.

Employing your Stress-Deflector Shield is about recognizing the onset of stress and having a ready set of activities to guide you back to tranquility. This approach keeps you afloat in life's turbulent waters, whether you're navigating them solo or with a partner who's just as keen to tackle the waves head-on.

3. The Joy Detective Being a Joy Detective is about donning your metaphorical magnifying glass and scouting out those hidden gems of happiness in the everyday. It's finding delight in the small things—a perfectly brewed cup of coffee, a surprise call from a friend, or the way your pet greets you like you're the best thing since sliced bread.

My Joy Jar sits on the kitchen counter, a constant reminder to look for the good. Each slip of paper represents a victory, a moment of gratitude. For those in relationships, sharing these discoveries helps create a culture of positivity that permeates your shared space. It's akin to compiling a highlight reel of your days, filled with snippets of laughter, triumphs, and even the bittersweet moments that, upon reflection, bring a smile.

Embracing the role of a Joy Detective means tuning into the frequency of positivity, even when static tries to drown it out. It's a practice that enriches your life, painting your days with strokes of joy, whether you're the sole artist or co-creating a masterpiece.

4. The Solo/Shared Success Dance The Solo/Shared Success Dance is your personal victory dance, a celebration of triumphs, whether they're shared or your own. It's acknowledging every step forward, every hurdle crossed. When you ace a presentation at work, celebrate with a little jig in your living room. When your partner nails their fitness goal, join them in a dance of triumph, transforming kitchen tiles into a disco floor.

The dance is more than just its movements. It's a celebration of the spirit behind them, a joyous ode to progress and a heartfelt testament to perseverance. Whether you're rocking out solo to your success playlist or waltzing around the living room with your partner, each step is a declaration: "We did it. I did it."

Embracing both solo and shared successes is about recognizing the individual and collective journeys. It's about being each other's cheerleader and also your own, celebrating life's achievements with a dance that's as unique as your journey.

5. The Adventure Attitude Adjustment The Adventure Attitude Adjustment is all about seeing life's unexpected turns as the beginning of a new adventure. It's the mindset that transforms a missed flight into

an unexpected night of exploration in a new city. It's looking at life's hiccups with a sense of curiosity and excitement, rather than dread.

For the solo adventurers, this might mean turning a job loss into an opportunity to travel or learn a new skill. In partnerships, transforming challenges into joint quests, such as impulsively adopting a pet tarantula, becomes an adventure filled with laughter and shared memories.

This attitude is about making 'lemonade out of lemons', but with a twist. It's a lemonade stand where you're experimenting with flavors, colors, and presentations. It's turning the mundane into the extraordinary, and the unexpected into an adventure. Whether you're dealing with these curveballs alone or with someone, the Adventure Attitude Adjustment is your ticket to enjoying the ride, no matter where the road takes you.

Alright, my intrepid explorers of life's grand tapestry, whether you're the lone ranger or part of a dynamic duo, we've navigated the treacherous yet thrilling waters of change together. With these five trusty strategies tucked into your belt, you're more than equipped to take on life's curveballs, be they wild pitches or gentle tosses. Grip your bat of resilience firmly, keep those eyes keen, and let's remember, those curveballs? They're not here to strike us out, but to test our swing, to refine our stance, and yes, sometimes to give us a tale that'll be told for ages.

As we stand on this base, ready to dash to the next, take a moment to relish in the journey thus far. You've ducked, you've dived, you've danced through the downpours and basked in the breakthroughs. Now, as we approach the new frontier of Chapter 6: "Step Six –

Letting Go of What No Longer Serves," we prepare to shed old skins, outdated modes, and burdensome weights. Embracing this process leads to a newfound lightness of being, filled with release and renewal.

So, take a deep breath, and let's leap together into the next chapter with the zest of a gazelle bounding across the savannah and the fierce heart of a champion who knows their worth. It's time to loosen our grips on the bats and gloves weighted with the past and reach for the future with open hands and hearts. Onward we march, to the rhythm of growth, to the beat of our own drum, to a chorus that sings of freedom and fresh starts. Swing at life with a wink, a nod, and perhaps a cheeky grin—because, my friends, we are in it to win it, come what may!

Step Six – Letting Go of What No Longer Serves

♥

"Letting go gives us freedom, and freedom is the only condition for happiness."

Imagine your life as a hot air balloon, all decked out and ready to parade across the sky. Except, there's a catch – it's still tethered to the ground by a bunch of ropes. These aren't just any ropes; they're the heavyweight champions of your past: grudges that could outlast fruitcake, fears that could star in their own horror movie, and loyalties that are more out of date than your high school yearbook photo. Now, I'll be the first to admit, letting go of these ropes can feel like trying to give a cat a bath – it's slippery, it's awkward, and you might get a few scratches in the process.

Here's the thing though – I've been there, standing in my metaphorical balloon basket, scissors in hand, wondering if I'll float or just flop.

For those riding solo, summoning the courage to cut ties with the 'me' you've outgrown is a crucial step in your personal evolution.

For the lovebirds, it's a two-person job where you take turns snipping away at the old baggage, hoping neither of you falls out of the basket in the process. I've learned it's less about the grand gesture of throwing ropes overboard and more about the quiet resolve to stop tripping over them.

Letting go involves acknowledging that these burdens, these ropes, have woven themselves into the landscape of your life. They're not lifelines but anchors. For me, realizing that holding onto a grudge was as useful as a chocolate teapot marked a turning point. And for you? It might mean understanding that freeing up space in your heart doesn't automatically invite loneliness; sometimes, it invites a whole new world of connections.

So, armed with humor as our shield and a healthy dose of self-deprecation as our spear, let's tackle this beast called 'letting go.' It's okay to acknowledge that the idea of freedom is as scary as it is exhilarating. But remember, every time we loosen a rope, we're not just setting ourselves free – we're giving our balloon a chance to find out just how high it can go. And hey, if we get a little more sky to dance in, a few more stars to wink at, well, that's just the universe's way of giving us a thumbs up.

Releasing Negative Cycles:

Okay, everyone, it's time for the grand premiere of 'Spot the Habit.' Imagine it's the least blockbuster game show where the prize is reclaiming your sanity. Picture this: your day is a canvas, and every habit is a stroke of paint. Some strokes contribute to a masterpiece, while others... well, let's just say they're more abstract chaos than Picasso. For instance, take my old habit of nodding along to every request like one of those dashboard bobbleheads. I said 'yes' so much, I could've been mistaken for a human echo.

Now, take a magnifying glass to your daily rituals. Do you see that habit of doom that keeps showing up uninvited? Maybe it's hitting snooze until you're doing a morning sprint worthy of the Olympics, or doomscrolling social media when you could be, I don't know, actually doing something you enjoy. These habits stick out like a sore thumb—or in my case, like a thumb that's volunteered to help everyone move their furniture.

Taking inventory is the next step. Sit down with a cup of coffee, or something stronger if necessary, and make a list. Write it all down, from the 3 PM chocolate raid to the 3 AM worry spiral. For me, the turning point was seeing my 'yes' habit in black and white, stretching out like a CVS receipt. That's when you realize your 'harmless' habits are actually clogging up your life like a bad plumbing job.

The next step extends beyond merely discarding that list. This phase involves actively observing these habits in their natural context, comprehending their patterns, and planning to subtly steer them towards a more manageable existence—or even show them the exit. I started by swapping out my knee-jerk 'yeses' for 'let me check my schedule' – a small change that turned my Tetris-block schedule into something vaguely resembling a normal calendar. It's about recognizing that every 'yes' to someone else often means a 'no' to your own peace of mind. So, let's get ready to turn those habits from persistent pests into extinct species, one 'Where's Waldo' stripe at a time.

1. Spot the Repeat Button My life was once a series of 'yes' echoes that left me stretched thinner than a budget yoga mat. Now, your mission—should you choose to accept it—is to play detective in your own life. Scrutinize your daily grind as if you're a sleuth in a noir film, looking for the patterns that keep popping up like uninvited guests.

You might find that you're the perennial people-pleaser or the late-night Netflix ninja. For me, it was the former, saying 'yes' when I really wanted to shout 'no', and watching my personal time vanish like a magician's assistant. The key here is observation without judgment. Sit with a notebook, jot down the habits as they occur, and soon you'll see the usual suspects revealing themselves.

Now, don't just stare at them in dismay; it's not a zoo exhibit. Under-stand their triggers—those moments when you automatically reach for the phone to agree to another favor or mindlessly open a social media app. It's time to recognize these patterns for what they are: the loops that keep you running on a hamster wheel of monotony.

With this newfound knowledge, prepare for change. It's like being at the helm of your ship, spotting the iceberg of 'yes' in the distance, and choosing to steer clear. As you become more aware of these repetitive habits, you'll feel empowered to start plotting a new course. It's the beginning of waving 'bye-bye' to the 'yes' and 'hello' to a life where you're the captain, not the cabin boy.

2. Chart the Fallout Once you've spotted the habits, it's time for a bit of damage assessment. Let's call it 'Chart the Fallout'. It's like an audit of your life, but instead of numbers, we're tallying the cost of your well-being. Those habitual 'yeses' may seem harmless at first glance,

but their cumulative effect is like a silent software update that's eating away at your bandwidth.

Take out your metaphorical clipboard and start tallying. Each 'yes' could be costing you a piece of your peace, or each snooze button slap could be stealing your morning serenity. My own habit of over-committing was like investing in stocks bound to plummet. I was bankrupting my downtime and my sleep was accruing interest in the form of dark under-eye circles.

It's not enough to recognize the cost; you've got to feel it. For every extra commitment I took on, I imagined a little of my life force draining away, like air from a tire. This part is crucial; it's the fuel for your desire to change. Write down not just the habit and its cost, but also how it makes you feel—exhausted, irritable, overwhelmed?

Now, use this ledger of losses to motivate your transformation. It's the evidence in the case against your current lifestyle. And as you start to realize just how much these habits are costing you, you'll begin to understand why change isn't just desirable—it's necessary. Your well-being is the currency you can't afford to waste.

3. Press Stop With the costs tallied, it's time for action—let's 'Press Stop'. Imagine your life as a movie that's been on a loop, playing the same scene over and over. It's worn out its welcome, and frankly, you're bored of it. That's where the big red stop button comes in. It's your veto power, your personal control to end the cycle.

or me, pressing stop was akin to assuming the role of gatekeeper over my time, discerning who and what merits entry. This shift entailed trading the instinctive 'yes' for a considered 'I'll get back to you,' allowing for a pause to weigh my commitments.' Start small; pick one pattern to interrupt and think of a practical alternative. It's like swapping out stale bread for fresh—it's the same sandwich, but oh, so much better.

This step is awkward at first, like learning a new dance move. You'll stumble, step on toes, maybe even face-plant. But it's all part of the process. I began rehearsing the word 'no' with my reflection and even my cat, building up the courage before I could assert it in a professional setting. This process was a rehearsal, repeating the line until it took on the ease of a well-practiced part. Here are some examples that show how to gracefully press 'stop' in scenarios with those close to you:

- The Overextended Invitation: When a dear friend or family member invites you to yet another event, and you're already stretched too thin, consider a response like, "I'm truly honored you thought of me, and I love spending time with you. Right now, my schedule is as packed as a holiday turkey. Can we find a time next month when I can give you my full attention?"

- The Favor Frenzy: If someone close asks for help when you're already overcommitted, try: "You know I'm your biggest fan, right? And I want to help in the way only a true fan would – effectively and wholeheartedly. At this moment, I'm swamped. Let's find a time when I can offer the support you deserve, without giving you half-baked help."

- The Persistent Project: Perhaps a loved one consistently seeks your input on a never-ending project. You might say, "I'm amazed by your dedication—it's like you're the Mozart of project planning! I need to tune my own life's symphony right now, so how about we set a specific time to brainstorm? This way, I can ensure I'm giving you the creativity you need from me."

- The Last-Minute Lifesaver: For those moments when you're asked to drop everything and rescue someone's crisis: "I see you're in a tough spot, and I want to throw you a lifeline. Right now, though, I'm underwater myself. Let's find another solution together, so we both stay afloat."

- The Constant Companion: If someone wants more of your time than you can give, consider: "Our time together is like a fine wine – it's precious and should be savored. I can't join you as often as we'd like, but when we do get together, let's make it memorable. Quality over quantity, right?"

In each of these examples, the key is to affirm the relationship, acknowledge the request, and offer an alternative that respects both your boundaries and the other person's feelings. It's about crafting responses that are as considerate and thoughtful as they are firm. This dance of diplomacy is the subtle art of pressing 'stop' while still playing the music of a caring relationship.

Remember, the objective is not to grind your life to a halt but to introduce pauses where you can steer in a new direction. It's okay to take a moment, breathe, and consult your inner compass. And when you're ready, with a deep breath and a clear head, hit that stop button. Your future self will thank you.

4. Find Your New Groove Stopping the old habit is only half the battle; now, it's time to 'Find Your New Groove'. Think of it as the soundtrack to your life; you've been playing the blues for too long, and

now it's time for some upbeat jazz. For me, it was about replacing 'yes' with activities that allowed me to reflect, like a walk in the park or a meditative cup of tea.

The aim here is to replace the negative habit with a positive one. If you're used to scrolling through social media first thing in the morning, try starting your day with a podcast or a chapter of a book. Make it something enjoyable, something that enriches rather than drains. Create new patterns that serve you, such as preparing breakfast the night before to allow for a calm start to your day instead of rushing through your morning routine.

This new habit should be a source of joy, not another chore. It should feel like slipping into a warm bath after a long day, not like squeezing into jeans that are two sizes too small. Choose something that aligns with your values and goals. If you're aiming for health, maybe it's a morning stretch instead of a sugar-laden coffee. If it's peace you seek, perhaps it's five minutes of gratitude journaling in place of doom-scrolling.

As you groove into your new habit, it'll start to feel like home. This new rhythm will become your default, the beat that your life dances to. And as you groove to this new beat, remember to be patient. It takes time to rewrite a soundtrack, but once you do, the melody of your life will be sweeter than ever.

5. Celebrate the Tiny Victories The final step in breaking free from negative cycles is to 'Celebrate the Tiny Victories'. Every time you successfully avoid the habitual pitfall, give yourself a round of applause, even if it's just mentally. I started with literal gold stars on a calendar; it was my way of saying, 'You did it, champ!'.

Celebrating these moments is like giving yourself a high five after a good run. It reinforces your new habits and turns the journey into something fun. It might be as simple as a happy dance after saying 'no', or treating yourself to a fancy coffee when you opt for a morning jog instead of a lie-in.

These mini-parties are the confetti in the parade of change. They make the process of transformation less daunting and more delightful. And don't worry about looking silly; if anything, it adds to the charm. Embrace the silly, embrace the fun, and most importantly, embrace the change.

Forgiving and Moving Forward:

Forgiveness, oh forgiveness—often tossed around like a frisbee at a family picnic, yet grasping it feels akin to catching said frisbee with greased-up hands. Let's demystify this slippery sucker and slice it into a five-step sandwich that's more digestible. This process is not a grandiose leap into oblivion accompanied by trumpets and fanfare; rather, it involves powering up the vacuum to clear away the dusty cobwebs that have settled in the attic of your mind.

Step one is spotting the grime. You have to pinpoint the exact spot where the dust bunnies of grudges are multiplying. Just like when I acknowledged that my perpetual annoyance at misplaced keys was actually frustration over misplaced trust in a friend. Shine a flashlight into the dark corners and see the clutter for what it is—a mess from the past that's cluttering up your present.

Next, we roll up our sleeves and decide to purge. This is the part where you commit to tossing out those old boxes labeled "Resentment" and "What-ifs." It's the mental equivalent of deciding, once and for all, to donate those bell-bottom jeans from high school you'll never wear again. Make the conscious decision to declutter your inner space. It doesn't have to be a grand gesture; even a small nod to let go can start the ball rolling down the hill of healing.

Now comes the actual cleaning—forgiveness in action. Imagine yourself with a mop and bucket, scrubbing away the stubborn stains of old hurts. It's not about erasing the past; it's about cleaning the slate so you're not constantly slipping on old issues. For me, it meant looking at an old betrayal and saying, "I choose to wipe away the hurt so I can walk safely forward." It's acknowledging that while the spill happened, you don't have to live with the stain forever.

Finally, once the floor is shiny and your attic is spacious, you take a moment to appreciate the clean expanse. This is where you invite in new, happier memories—like hanging up pictures of good times and achievements. Make a conscious effort to replace the spaces where grudges once lurked with positive affirmations and joyful recollections. Make peace with the past not just to 'move on,' but to clear a space for new, beautiful experiences waiting just outside your freshly polished window.

1. **Name That Tune of Hurt.** The key to turning the page on past hurts begins with a simple, yet profound, realization: the recurring themes of discomfort in our lives are often echoes of deeper wounds. It's akin to hearing a familiar tune that brings a sense of unease, yet we find ourselves unable to stop humming along. For me, it struck during those mundane moments of daily life, like the acrid smell of burnt toast that suddenly became a stark reminder of relationships that had similarly gone up in smoke. This epiphany was neither pleasant nor easy, but it was necessary.

In the quiet aftermath of this revelation, I understood that recognizing these patterns was only the prelude. The real challenge lay in delving into the lyrics of my life's song, the verses etched with pain, and daring to rewrite them. It was time to confront the underlying hurt—not with the intention of erasing it, but with the purpose of understanding its melody. Acknowledging the pain was like tuning an instrument, ensuring that the notes of my past experiences resonated with clarity rather than dissonance.

As the process unfolded, I learned that naming my hurt wasn't just about assigning blame or dredging up old regrets. It was about taking control of the narrative, shifting from a passive listener to an active composer of my life's soundtrack. With each piece of hurt I named, I found the strength to gently lift the needle from the groove of past grievances and set it down on a new track. This shift didn't happen overnight—it was a gradual process, much like a composer refining a symphony, note by note, until the music finally feels right.

Embrace this journey by allowing yourself to feel the full range of emotions that accompany each painful memory. Give yourself permission to pause the hurtful track, examine it, and then, with intention, choose to fill the silence with a rhythm that uplifts and heals. This transformation doesn't invalidate the past; instead, it weaves the old melodies into a richer, more harmonious composition. It's a symphony of forgiveness, self-discovery, and ultimately, self-love—a melody that plays on, lighter and more hopeful with every beat.

2. The Decision Detox Choosing to forgive is kind of like deciding to swap out those old, holey undies for a fresh, snazzy pair. It's not that the old ones didn't serve a purpose—they covered the essentials—but let's be honest, they had about as much support as a limp noodle. The

decision to detox your emotional wardrobe is admitting that maybe, just maybe, you're due for an upgrade. It's looking at the grudge you've been nursing like a pet rock and realizing it doesn't even sparkle.

Kicking off this detox is no stroll through a fragrant meadow. It's more like the first jog after a Netflix marathon; you're gasping for air, wondering why on Earth you're doing this to yourself. You stand in front of the mirror, give yourself a pep talk, and commit to this mental flush. You declare, "Out with the sour lemons of resentment, in with the lemonade of letting go," because you know deep down, it's time for something sweeter.

As you commit to this detox, you'll notice it's a bit like peeling an onion. There are layers upon layers of feels, and yes, there might be tears. But between the sniffles and the soul-searching, you'll find moments of unexpected hilarity—like realizing that half your grudges are as outdated as a flip phone. And when the air clears, there's this sense of 'aha', as if your emotional GPS just recalculated a faster route to Peaceville.

Let's break down the "How" of this whole forgiveness detox with some actionable steps:

- Set the Stage for Sincerity: Start by creating a space that feels safe and comfortable for this emotional deep dive. Maybe it's your favorite armchair with the cozy throw, or a spot in the park where the squirrels are the only eavesdroppers. You want a place where you can be honest with yourself without distractions or judgments. It's your personal truth booth.

- The Reflective Rundown: Grab a notebook—any old notebook will do, though something with unicorns on the cover might add a touch of whimsy to the process. Now, write down the grievances you're carrying. But here's the twist: for every annoyance or hurt, find a funny or absurd angle. Did someone steal your parking spot? Write a mock epic battle poem about it. Try acknowledging the pain while also diffusing it with humor.

• Speak the Language of Self-Compassion: As you list these old wounds, talk to yourself like you're a stand-up comic gently roasting a beloved friend. Use humor to soften the edges. For instance, if you're ruminating on a breakup, you might say, "I gave them the best years of my hair!" Find lightness in the dark spots.

• The Ritual of Release: Create a forgiveness ritual that feels right for you. This could be as simple as saying out loud, "I forgive you, you clueless cupcake," or as elaborate as writing down your resentments and then shredding the paper while doing your best evil laugh. The point is to make the act of letting go both meaningful and slightly ridiculous to take the sting out of it.

• Reinforce with Repetition: Just like a sitcom catchphrase becomes funnier with repetition, so too can your process of forgiveness. Come back to your list and your self-talk regularly. Notice if there's a little less charge each time, a little more room for a chuckle. Over time, the repetition not only reinforces your new mindset but also turns the act of forgiveness into a habit, as comfortable and familiar as your favorite sitcom.

- Seek External Levity: Sometimes, sharing your journey with a trusted friend can inject an extra dose of humor. They might offer a perspective that turns a mountain back into a molehill. Just like a sitcom benefits from a good ensemble cast, your forgiveness process might benefit from a few supporting characters.

- Celebrate the Small Wins: Got through a whole day without mentally replaying that awkward conversation from five years ago? That's a win! Celebrate with something that brings you joy, whether it's a dance to your victory song or treating yourself to a piece of that fancy chocolate you hide from everyone else.

Remember, forgiveness is a process, not a one-time event. It's about gradually shifting your perspective until one day, you realize the weight you've been carrying has turned into a collection of funny anecdotes. It's not about erasing history; it's about rewriting the story in which you're the hero who overcomes with a smile and possibly, a well-timed joke.

Sure, some days you'll slip. You'll glance at that pile of old resentments and think, "Maybe just one more spiteful stew." But then you remember the taste of freedom—a flavor so bold it makes your previous diet of bitterness taste as bland as cardboard. So, you double down, toss out the stale grievances, and stock your shelves with forgiveness-flavored goodies. Each little 'aha' moment, each chuckle at the absurdity of what you used to carry, becomes a celebration of your newfound lightness.

By the time you're through, your emotional kitchen is sparkling, and you're serving up dishes of understanding and self-compassion that are five-star worthy. This detox process goes beyond forgetting past mistakes; it transforms them into a series of comic missteps from which you emerge, not merely unharmed, but with a sense of pride and a smile. Discover that the true reward is the freedom to laugh at your previous hang-ups, which adds the finishing touch to your journey of forgiveness.

The Decision Detox:

Choosing to forgive is akin to deciding on a cleanse for your emotional well-being. It's not about purging memories or people from your life, but rather detoxifying the impact they have on you. Think of it like replacing your daily caffeine with a nourishing smoothie; it may not give you the immediate buzz, but it enriches you in more sustainable ways. This choice to forgive might start with a simple declaration to yourself in the mirror, affirming your decision to let go of bitterness. It's about pouring out the stale resentment that's been sitting at the bottom of your heart and refilling it with fresh, clean compassion—not just for others, but for yourself. With each step towards forgiveness, you're cleansing your palate of the past, making room for new, more delightful flavors of life.

Resentment Release Valve:

Resentment, that sly squatter in the rooms of our minds, can stack up like a collection of bricks in a backpack we never intended to carry. It begins with a small annoyance, a minor grievance, easily shrugged off. But then comes another, and another, until the weight bows our shoulders and sours our spirits. We trudge through our days, backs bent, spirits weary, often forgetting why we started carrying them in the first place. It's a silent burden that can turn the lightest feet into leaden stompers, transforming sprints of joy into marathons of endurance.

Every brick in that backpack has a history, a story, a reason for being there. They're the remnants of conflicts unresolved, of words that cut deeper than we admitted, of apologies we never received—or gave. They're tangible tokens of disappointments and betrayals, a collection of 'what ifs' and 'if onlys'. With each new addition, the weight increases, and the memory of moving freely, of laughing with ease, grows dim. We convince ourselves that this is just how life is—hard, heavy, a relentless uphill climb. Yet, in the quiet moments, we can't help but wonder what it would be like to set that backpack down, even just for a moment.

And here's the kicker: that backpack, with its cumbersome load, is not strapped to us by anyone's hand but our own. We are the keepers of the keys to those locks, the architects of our encumbrances. It's an empowering, if daunting, realization. The bricks of resentment are not immovable. They are not irremovable. They are choices. To continue carrying them is a choice. To set them down, examine them, and ultimately, let them go, is also a choice—one that leads to a lighter journey, an easier laugh, and a freedom we might have thought we'd lost. So, let's explore how to unpack that heavy load, brick by brick, and rediscover the spring in our step that life's burdens have pressed flat.

Let's break it down into five actionable steps:

1. Inventory Check: First up, it's time for a little honesty hour

with your backpack. Lay out all those metaphorical bricks and see what's written on them. I had to confront a brick labeled 'Betrayal' from an old business partner. It's about recognizing each resentment for what it is and deciding it's time they stopped taking up space in your life.

2. Weight Assessment: Now, pick up each brick and feel its weight. What has lugging around this resentment cost you? Has it strained relationships? Has it robbed you of peace? For me, each resentment brick was a night of lost sleep, a day of distracted work, and an ounce of joy gone. Acknowledge the cost.

3. The Unloading Process: This is where you decide to offload those bricks. It might mean a conversation, a letter never sent, or a symbolic gesture like throwing pebbles into a lake, each one representing a resentment you're letting go of. Releasing burdens goes further than simply letting them fall; it involves a deliberate choice to leave them behind and move forward.

4. Step Into Lightness: With the bricks gone, take a moment to feel the difference. Walk around. Take a deep breath. Do you feel that? It's called freedom. Suddenly, your shoulders aren't so hunched. There's a spring in your step. I remember the first time I walked without my backpack of grudges – it was like rediscovering how to move.

5. Maintenance: Keeping the backpack empty is a daily task. Every evening, do a quick check. If you find a new brick has sneaked in there, address it before it settles in. Maybe

it's jotting down a worry and then ripping the paper up, or visualizing a concern melting away with each exhale of a deep breath.

Releasing resentment isn't just an act; it's a transformative process—a kind of spring cleaning of the soul. It's an art, really, in which you become both the sculptor and the marble, chipping away at the heavy excess until what's left is something lighter, more genuine. It begins with a choice, a conscious decision to stop the collection of emotional detritus before it starts to pile up. Choosing to leave behind that unappealing souvenir is akin to discerning what aligns with your inner harmony and what disrupts it.

But, let's be honest, sometimes those bricks find their way into our mental space without us even noticing. They slip in quietly, like uninvited guests at a party, and before we know it, they're munching away at our happiness, taking up space on our favorite emotional couch. When that happens, when we find ourselves unwitting curators of a gallery of grievances, it's time to roll up our sleeves and get to work. We have to sort through them, examine them, understand why we let them in, and most importantly, how we can show them the door. It's not about a frantic purge; it's a methodical process, requiring patience, self-compassion, and a steady hand.

The act of letting go, brick by brick, is not always easy. It's a gentle but firm negotiation between the heart and mind, a balancing act of acknowledging the weight of each resentment and understanding the relief of setting it down. It's a gradual journey back to lightness, to the days when our internal landscape was a meadow of possibility, not a warehouse of woes. With each brick released, the horizon of our spirit expands, the sky of our potential brightens, and we rediscover the paths of joy that were there all along, just waiting for us to take the first step.

Grow a Garden of New Thoughts:

In the garden of the mind, every thought is a seed, and old grudges are like weeds that choke out the life of the more desirable blooms. When we pull these weeds, what we're left with is not a barren plot, but a rich soil ripe for planting. It's an empty canvas beckoning for a stroke of green, a promise of what can flourish there. The act of planting new seeds of affirmation is both literal and symbolic; it's deciding that where doubt once grew like dandelions, now will stand the sturdy oaks of self-assurance and the delicate blossoms of hope.

Watering these seeds is an act of commitment, a daily practice that requires us to nourish these nascent thoughts with actions that validate our self-worth. It might be as simple as standing in front of the mirror every morning, affirming your strengths, or as complex as setting and achieving small goals that reaffirm your capabilities. Each positive action is a drop of water, each word of encouragement a ray of sun, collectively transforming the seeds into sprouts that reach upwards towards the light.

As these new thoughts take root, you'll witness a transformation that's as dramatic as any spring bloom. The barren patches of your psyche will give way to lush greenery, a mental landscape that's both pleasing to the eye and soul. Confidence and contentment will no longer be rare blossoms, but perennial features of your garden, perking up even on the cloudiest of days. This is the power of cultivating a positive mindset; it changes not just the way you think, but the way you feel and act.

But a garden, no matter how beautiful, requires upkeep. You must tend to it, pruning the withered branches of negativity, those dry twigs of self-doubt that can sap the energy from the healthiest of thoughts. It's an ongoing process, identifying the negative patterns that creep back in, and snipping them away before they can take hold again. And as you do, you'll find yourself not just a gardener, but a connoisseur of your own mental landscape, appreciating the richness of growth that comes from within.

Creating a vibrant garden of positive thoughts requires consistent, intentional actions. Here are some concrete steps you can take to foster this growth:

- Seed Selection: Take an honest look at the garden of your mind. What thoughts and beliefs have been taking root? Just like choosing seeds for a garden, decide which positive thoughts you want to cultivate. Identify the affirmations that will counter the negativity.

- Soil Preparation: Before planting new seeds, you need good soil. Prepare your mind by clearing out the old, limiting beliefs.

This could involve reflection, meditation, or even therapy—whatever helps you to break up the hard soil of old patterns and make room for new growth.

- Planting the Seeds: Now it's time to plant. Introduce your chosen affirmations into your daily routine. Place them where you'll see them: on your phone, your fridge, your workspace.

Begin each day by affirming these new beliefs. Water them with attention and care.

- Daily Tending: Every garden needs regular care. Nurture your growing thoughts with daily actions that align with your affirmations.

This might involve setting small goals, practicing gratitude, or taking moments throughout the day to reinforce your new mindset.

- Weeding and Protecting: Be vigilant about weeds, which can be old patterns trying to creep back in. When you notice a negative thought, gently remove it and re-affirm your positive intention.

Protect your new garden by surrounding yourself with positive influences and avoiding situations that may reintroduce the weeds.

- Enjoying the Blooms: Take time to appreciate the new growth in your mind's garden. Notice how your new thoughts affect your feelings and actions.

Celebrate the small victories that come from having a healthier mindset. Maybe it's feeling calmer in a situation that used to stress you out or making a decision that reflects your new affirmations.

- Ongoing Cultivation: A garden is never really "finished." Continue to cultivate your thoughts, introduce new affirmations as you grow, and adjust your routine to accommodate life's changes. Regularly take stock of your internal garden, and feel proud of the lush landscape you've created within your mind.

By following these steps, you're committing to a process of continual growth and renewal. It's a journey that transforms not just your internal world but will begin to reflect in your external life as well, bringing a harvest of happiness, peace, and fulfillment. Basking in the beauty of a mind in full bloom isn't an end, but a continuous journey. It's sitting in the midst of your mental oasis, taking in the vibrant colors, the scents, the symphony of the birds, and knowing that it's all a reflection of you. It's the ultimate reward for the hard work of letting go, for the daily toil of nurturing positivity, and for the courage to plant new seeds even when the frost of past pains seemed unyielding. In this garden, contentment doesn't just visit; it lives, it thrives, and it invites others to enjoy its splendor.

The Celebration Shindig:

Throwing a Celebration Shindig is indeed a unique form of personal acknowledgment. It's like giving yourself a high-five for crossing an emotional finish line. When you choose to let go of the past and forgive, you're not just saying goodbye to old resentments; you're welcoming a new chapter of your life. It's a moment worth marking.

For me, it started with recognizing that each act of forgiveness was a milestone. Just like a runner feels a surge of accomplishment with every lap, I realized that forgiving was my emotional marathon. I didn't need streamers or a crowd; I needed to honor the quiet victories that no one saw – the hard-fought battles within the confines of my own heart. It was about giving myself permission to feel proud, to acknowledge that while the journey was mine alone, it was no less significant.

So, here's to the Celebration Shindig – the personal party that doesn't require a venue, guest list, or even an occasion outfit. It could be as simple as taking a moment to sit in silence, savoring the stillness that comes from shedding emotional baggage. Or it might be indulging in a small treat, a physical manifestation of the sweetness of moving on. When I reached a point of forgiveness, I marked it with a solo dance in my living room, my feet thumping to the rhythm of newfound freedom. It's these simple, solitary celebrations that stitch together to form the tapestry of our healed selves.

Now, let's delve into how you can throw your own shindig, step by step:

- Recognition Over Revelry: Start by recognizing the significance of what you've accomplished. Forgiveness isn't easy; it's a profound shift in perspective and deserves to be honored. You could write a letter to yourself, detailing the journey you've been on, the challenges you've faced, and the growth that has resulted. It's about putting into words the intangible, celebrating the invisible work that's been done.

- Personal Party Planning: Plan your celebration in a way that feels meaningful to you. It doesn't need to be extravagant; it should be reflective of your personality and preferences. If you're an introvert, maybe you create a quiet ritual, lighting a candle, playing your favorite song, and taking a moment to reflect in solitude. If you're more extroverted, perhaps you gather a few close friends for a dinner where you share your experiences and toast to future happiness.

- Joyful Activities: Choose activities that fill you with joy and signify the new chapter you're entering. This could be as simple as watching the sunrise to welcome the new dawn of your life without the burden of resentment. I remember taking that bike ride, feeling the wind against my face, and realizing it was a metaphor for the fresh breeze of forgiveness blowing through my life.

• Sharing the Success: If your journey of forgiveness involved others, consider sharing your celebration with them. It could be a way to acknowledge the role they played and the support they provided. When I reached a significant milestone of forgiveness with a family member, we celebrated over a meal. It was an act of communal joy, a shared acknowledgment that we were moving forward together.

• Making It a Tradition: Make these celebrations a tradition. Every time you reach a new milestone in personal growth, take the time to celebrate. Over time, these celebrations will form a tapestry of moments that remind you of your resilience and capacity for change. They become markers on the timeline of your life, each one a testament to your ability to adapt and find joy.

Welcoming moments of celebration into your life goes beyond simply reveling in victories; it involves establishing a foundation in the renewed self that rises from previous experiences. It's a toast to the resilience that's carried you through the storms and a nod to the peace you've earned. Each celebration is a stone laid on the path of your continued journey, a journey marked not by the distance traveled but by the growth along the way. It's taking the time to acknowledge that yes, it was hard, but here you are, on the other side, perhaps a little weary but wiser and more whole.

As you weave these celebrations into the fabric of your daily life, you're not just commemorating victories; you're reinforcing the positive changes you've painstakingly implemented. It's like building a monument within, one that stands in honor of your fortitude and grace. These moments are your personal festivals, each one a tribute to a battle fought and a reminder that the future is a canvas waiting for the bright colors of your transformed spirit. Remember, it was you who took the scattered pieces and built something beautiful.

So, when you give yourself permission to celebrate, it's not frivolous; it's fundamental. It could be as simple as a quiet evening with a book that makes your heart sing, or as lively as a solo kitchen dance party to your favorite tune. It's the solitary high-five after a day of hard-earned self-care, the silent acknowledgment of your strength as you drift off to sleep. These acts of celebration are the soft exhalations of a being learning to love itself fiercely, fully, and without reservation.

And as you do this, understand that celebrating isn't just a part of the healing process; it is the beautiful outcome of it. It's the full-circle moment where you can look back not in anger or sorrow, but with a gentle smile for the person you were and a sparkling toast to the person you are becoming. It's the realization that healing isn't just about getting better from past wounds; it's about embracing life with a vigor and joy that was perhaps previously unknown to you. So go ahead, celebrate your heart out, because each moment of joy is a declaration that you are moving forward, unwaveringly, into a life that's brimming with possibility.

Creating Space for New Love:

When I decided it was time to make a change in my life, the first thing I did was take a brutally honest inventory of my daily habits. I noticed that I had a tendency to hold onto past mistakes and slip-ups, replaying them in my mind like a blooper reel that just wouldn't stop. It was time to stop this cycle, to stop being my own toughest critic.

I started by setting aside a little time each day for reflection. Not to dwell on what went wrong, but to acknowledge it and then consciously shift my focus to what I could do better moving forward. I made a simple list of things that I wanted to change, like being more patient or less quick to judge, and I pinned it on my fridge. It was a daily reminder that I was working towards becoming a better version of myself.

Next, I worked on changing my reactions. Instead of getting frustrated over little setbacks or snapping at loved ones over trivial matters, I practiced taking a deep breath and responding with calmness. It wasn't easy, and I slipped up plenty of times, but the important thing was that I kept trying, each time responding a little better than the last.

I also reached out to friends and family, telling them about my journey towards personal growth. Sharing my goals made them feel more tangible and also gave me a support network that held me accountable. We often think that admitting we want to change is a sign of weakness, but in my experience, it's been the complete opposite. It's empowering.

Finally, I celebrated the small victories along the way. Each time I managed to break a negative cycle, I'd do something small but meaningful to acknowledge my progress, like treating myself to a coffee from my favorite cafe or enjoying an extra hour of sleep on a Saturday morning.

These straightforward steps didn't transform my life overnight, but they did set me on a path towards ongoing improvement. And that's what matters most—not the speed of change, but the direction.

Emotional Spring Cleaning: Just like tidying up a cluttered room can bring a sense of peace, cleaning up our emotional landscape is equally cathartic. It's about looking within and recognizing the feelings and memories that have overstayed their welcome. So how do you begin? Start by taking stock of your emotions and identifying those that are no longer serving you. Reflect on each one, and ask yourself whether it contributes to your growth or holds you back. This process can be as simple as writing down thoughts and feelings that arise throughout the day and assessing their impact on your well-being. The goal here is not to judge yourself but to become more aware of your emotional inventory.

Emotional Spring Cleaning isn't just about a one-off decluttering session; it's an ongoing process of introspection and renewal. Here's a step-by-step approach to make this concept a practical part of your daily routine:

1. Inventory of Emotions: Begin by creating an emotional inventory. This means taking a moment each day to write down your feelings and experiences. It can be in a journal, on your phone, or even scraps of paper. The medium isn't as important as the action. Write down everything from the trivial annoyances to the deeper, more complex emotions. This inventory will serve as the foundation for your emotional spring cleaning, giving you a clear picture of your current emotional state.

2. Emotional Sorting: Once you've taken stock, it's time to sort through your emotional inventory. Just as you would separate items to keep, donate, or throw away when tidying a room, do the same with your feelings. Which emotions are beneficial and contribute positively to your life? Which ones have become burdensome? Sorting can help you identify patterns and triggers, allowing you to understand what emotions are worth holding onto and which ones need to be released.

3. Reflection and Decision Making: With your emotions sorted, reflect on each one. Why do you feel this way? Is this emotion based on a current situation, or is it a residual feeling from the past? Decide which emotions you want to keep and nurture and which ones you're ready to let go of. This step is crucial because it empowers you to take control of your emotional well-being.

4. Conscious Release: For those emotions that no longer serve you, consciously choose to release them. This can be done through various methods such as meditation, visualization, or even physical activities like exercise or art. Find what works for you—a method that allows you to feel a sense of letting go. It might feel awkward or forced at first, but with practice, it becomes a powerful tool for emotional liberation.

5. Regular Maintenance: Finally, just like any form of spring cleaning, regular maintenance is key. Make this emotional check-in a part of your daily or weekly routine. It prevents the build-up of emotional clutter and helps you stay on top of your emotional well-being. Over time, this practice will not only clear out the old but also make space for new, more positive emotions and experiences to take root.

By incorporating these practical steps into your life, emotional spring cleaning can become a transformative practice that consistently refreshes and revitalizes your inner world.

Open the Doors:

Once you've done some emotional decluttering, it's time to open yourself up to new experiences. This means stepping out of your comfort zone and trying things that you wouldn't normally consider. Say 'yes' to that invitation you'd typically turn down, start a conversation with someone new, or pick up a hobby you've always been curious about. Opening the doors to new experiences can lead to growth, learning, and an expanded sense of self. Be proactive in seeking out opportunities that align with your values and interests.

Opening up to new experiences brings a thrilling mix of excitement and challenge, embracing the unknown and welcoming fresh opportunities with enthusiasm. Here are some practical steps to help guide you through this process:

1. Redefine Your Comfort Zone: Your comfort zone is a behavioral space where activities and behaviors fit a routine and pattern that minimizes stress and risk. The first step to opening new doors is redefining the boundaries of your comfort zone. Start small. If the idea of attending a large social gathering is intimidating, begin with something less daunting, like joining an online forum or attending a webinar in an area of interest.

2. Accept Invitations: When an opportunity arises, say 'yes' more often. Whether it's an invitation to a virtual book club, a socially-distanced walk with a neighbor, or a new project at work, accepting these invitations can lead to unexpected joys and learning opportunities.

Remember, every big tree once sprouted from a tiny seed of opportunity.

3. Initiate New Interactions: Don't wait for others to come to you. Be the initiator of new interactions. This could be as simple as striking up a conversation with someone in line at the grocery store or reaching out to an acquaintance on social media. These small acts of initiation often open doors to new friendships and experiences.

4. Explore New Hobbies: Pick a hobby or activity you've always been interested in but never pursued. This could be anything from learning a musical instrument, trying your hand at painting, or even starting a garden. Hobbies not only enrich your life with new skills and passions but also have the power to connect you with like-minded individuals.

5. Be Proactive Online: In today's digital age, the world is at your fingertips. Utilize online platforms to explore subjects you're curious about. Join webinars, enroll in online courses, or start a blog. The digital world offers countless avenues to expand your horizons right from the comfort of your home.

6. Volunteer: Offering your time to a cause can be a great way to open up to new experiences. Volunteering allows you to meet people from diverse backgrounds, learn new skills, and contribute to something larger than yourself. It's a fulfilling way to open doors you didn't even know existed.

7. Reflect and Adjust: As you try new things, take time to reflect on these experiences. How do they align with your values and interests? Use this reflection to make adjustments, either by continuing to explore further or by closing the door and seeking new paths. This re-

flective practice ensures that the new doors you open lead to fulfilling and enriching experiences.

Embarking on the path to new experiences is like beginning a new chapter in the grand book of your life. Each step outside your usual routine can unfurl a scroll of uncharted territory, ripe with the potential for growth and learning. By courageously stepping through new doors, you're not just dipping your toes into unfamiliar waters; you're diving into a sea of possibilities that can profoundly shape your character and outlook. This deliberate action to widen your horizon is not merely about collecting experiences as if they were souvenirs, but about enriching the tapestry of your life with vibrant threads of diversity.

With each new endeavor, you challenge the status quo of your comfort zone, stretching it to accommodate more of the world's vastness within it. This isn't just about ticking boxes on a bucket list or filling a social calendar; it's a transformative journey that beckons you to evolve with every new encounter. As you say 'yes' to new opportunities, start conversations with unfamiliar faces, or immerse yourself in novel hobbies, you are actively constructing a more complex, insightful, and open version of yourself. It's a process that polishes the lens through which you view the world, allowing you to appreciate its myriad colors and contours with greater clarity and understanding.

Thus, as you adopt this mindset of openness, you're not just opening doors; you're also setting the stage for serendipity to walk into your life. Each new experience has the potential to change the narrative of your existence in ways you might never have imagined. It's about living your life as an ever-expanding story where every chapter offers its own adventures, lessons, and memories. And remember, as you turn each page with anticipation, it's the unexpected plot twists that often lead to the most memorable tales. So keep turning those doorknobs, and let each opened door reveal a new horizon, a new perspective, and a new you.

Nurture the New:

Finally, as you welcome new experiences and emotions into your life, it's crucial to nurture them. Pay attention to what brings you joy and fulfillment and invest time and energy into these areas. Perhaps you've discovered a newfound passion for painting, or you've started to form meaningful connections in a community group. Whatever it is, give these new aspects of your life the care they deserve. This might involve setting aside time each day or week to engage with these interests, or it could mean continuing education in a particular area to deepen your understanding and skills.

Nurturing the new facets of your life is akin to tending a garden you've just planted. It's not enough to simply plant the seeds; you must also water them, give them enough sunlight, and protect them from the weeds. Here are five practices to help you cultivate the new passions and connections you've found:

1. **Scheduled Cultivation**: Set aside dedicated time in your daily or weekly schedule to engage with your new interests. Cultivating personal growth could mean dedicating an hour to painting post-dinner or regularly attending community gatherings, thereby integrating these activities firmly into your daily life. Think of it as an appointment with your future self, one where you show up with the same seriousness as you would for a business meeting or doctor's appointment.

By doing this, you give your new pursuits the space to evolve from passing interests to integral parts of your life.

2. **Skill Sharpening:** Invest in continuous learning and improvement. If you've taken up painting, for example, consider taking classes to refine your technique, or if you're part of a book club, read extra material on the author or genre to bring richer insights into discussions. The investment in education need not be formal; it could be as informal as watching tutorial videos online or attending workshops. The key is to approach your new interests with a student's mindset, always open and eager to learn more and do better. This not only enhances your skills but also keeps the flame of passion for your new interest alive and burning brightly.

3. **Social Integration:** Connect with like-minded individuals who share your interests. This could mean joining online forums, local clubs, or community groups where ideas and enthusiasm are exchanged. Surrounding yourself with a community not only provides motivation but also introduces different perspectives that can enhance your own experience. It's also a reminder that you're not alone on this journey of discovery; there's a whole tribe of people out there who can support and inspire you.

4. **Reflective Practice:** Take time to reflect on what you're learning and experiencing. This could be through journaling, meditative practices, or simply having deep conversations with friends or mentors about your journey. Reflection allows you to digest and internalize your experiences, turning them from mere activities into meaningful parts of your life

story. It helps you understand not just the 'how' but also the 'why' behind your interests, which deepens your connection to them.

5. **Celebratory Milestones**: Celebrate your milestones, no matter how small they may seem. Finished your first painting? Hang it up. Read your first book in a new genre? Share your thoughts on it with friends or on social media. These celebrations are affirmations of your progress and serve as motivational bookmarks in your life's narrative. They remind you of where you started and how far you've come, and they set the stage for all the accomplishments yet to come.

Embracing new interests and skills with the intent of weaving them into the fabric of your life requires more than just a fleeting engagement; it demands a deeper integration. When you consciously decide to include these practices into your daily life, you are committing to a journey of continuous growth and enrichment. It's the difference between skimming the surface of a hobby and diving into it as a part of your identity. This integration is a deliberate process, a choice to not just entertain these interests when convenient but to give them a permanent home in your schedule and in your heart.

As these practices become part of your routine, they evolve from mere activities into key components that contribute to your overall well-being. They begin to shape your days, influence your thoughts, and color your conversations. The joy found in painting, the insights gained from community discussions, or the satisfaction from mastering a new language start to thread through the narrative of your life. They become topics of interest that you share with others, sources of inspiration during challenging times, and the backdrop of your quiet moments of reflection. The value of these interests is amplified when they are no longer just things you do, but rather, they become ways you experience and interpret the world.

The transformation from a passing interest to a core aspect of your life doesn't happen overnight. It's a gradual process that's built on each day's small decisions to engage, learn, and celebrate. Over time, the cumulative effect of these decisions is significant. Your life becomes richer, more colorful, and deeply satisfying. You become a person with diverse passions, a wide range of skills, and a life that is as interesting and multi-faceted as the interests you pursue. This is the beauty of fully integrating your new pursuits into your life: they contribute to the wonderful complexity that makes you uniquely you.

As we close the chapter on freeing ourselves from the burdens of the past and embracing new chapters, it's vital to recognize that this is not the end but a beginning. Every step in the process of release and embracing new experiences enriches life with added vibrancy and color. We carry forward the lessons learned, draw upon the strength we've garnered, and infuse each new day with the joy we've unearthed. The past, with all its lessons, is a foundation, not a prison, and the future is a canvas, awaiting the colors we choose to paint with from our renewed palette.

Now, as we turn the page to Chapter 7, we carry with us the lightness of being that comes from unburdened hearts and open minds. We've decluttered the old, made space for the new, and now it's time to explore the next phase of our journey: the art of maintaining this newfound freedom and happiness. Chapter 7 will guide us in solidifying these changes into lasting habits, ensuring that the doors we've opened remain wide, welcoming continuous growth and love. It's about sustaining the balance, nurturing the growth, and weaving the fabric of our lives into a tapestry that truly reflects who we are and aspire to be.

Step Seven – Celebrating Love Every Day

♥

"In the arithmetic of love, one plus one equals everything, and two minus one equals nothing."

Ah, the grand finale, the last chapter in our journey through the labyrinth of love. Here we stand, at the threshold of daily celebration, ready to wrap up the gift that is affection and connection. This isn't the kind of present you unwrap in a flurry of excitement and then forget about; it's the sort of treasure that you keep unwrapping, day by day, finding new depths and joys in its layers. In the arithmetic of love, the sum is indeed greater than its parts, a formula where "one plus one equals everything, and two minus one equals nothing."

Love is the quiet morning rituals, the shared glances over cups of coffee, and the comfort found in the familiarity of a shared life. It's in the soft silence between words, the gentle tug of a smile, and the warmth of a hand search for yours across the couch. It's not reserved for the crescendos of grand romantic gestures, nor is it confined to the anniversary dates marked in bold on the calendar. Instead, it's in the everyday mundanities, the ebb and flow of the quotidian tide that sweeps through our lives.

Yet, even as we acknowledge love's omnipresence, it's easy to let it slip into the backdrop, like the habitual hum of a refrigerator or the steady tick of a clock. We must, therefore, make a conscious effort to keep it in our line of sight, to celebrate it with the same fervor with which we would our most significant achievements. Pouring ourselves a cup of wisdom means recognizing that the simplest acts of love can be the most profound. It's understanding that in the grand equation of our lives, the constants of care and commitment are what balance the variables of chaos and change.

As we sip on the rich brew of companionship, let us be reminded that love, much like our daily coffee, is a choice, a ritual, and a small act of rebellion against the solitude of existence. It is a deliberate pause in the rush of days to savor the flavor of togetherness, to bask in the aroma of mutual respect and affection. The decision to love each day is a testament to the human spirit's resilience and its eternal search for connection.

So here we are, at the end yet beginning anew each day, toasting to the constancy and the certainty that in the complex math of human emotions, love is the one equation that we all strive to balance. As we turn this page and look to the chapters that follow, let us carry with us the lessons learned, the laughter shared, and the love celebrated in the quiet corners of every day. For in the end, it is these moments that make up the story of our lives, written in the ink of love, bound in the book of time.

Practicing Daily Gratitude:

Gratitude doesn't require grand gestures or perfectly penned prose; it thrives on authenticity and the quiet recognition of life's smaller gifts. It's like those moments when you're hit with a sudden rush of warmth from a memory, a kind word, or a shared laugh—unremarkable to the world, perhaps, but deeply significant to you. These instances are like hidden treasures in the sand, and acknowledging them doesn't mean you need a metal detector; all it takes is a moment of mindful pause.

Think about it: how often do we breeze past the little conveniences and joys that stitch our days together without a second thought? The silent hum of your fridge keeping your food fresh, the dependable old boots that keep your feet dry, the spontaneous hug from your child, or even the smooth functioning of your favorite app—these are the unsung heroes in the narrative of our daily lives. Recognizing these might not create a seismic shift in your day, but, much like a subtle seasoning brings out the flavor in a dish, they enhance the overall taste of our existence.

So here's the nitty-gritty of everyday gratitude: spot the good stuff amid the mundane. Like a mental snapshot of your dog's goofy grin or the comfortable silence shared with a friend. It's the internal 'thank you' that bubbles up when you catch the bus just in time, or when the Wi-Fi works without a hitch during an important call. It's the mental tick mark next to the moments that make you unconsciously nod in silent appreciation.

Incorporating this kind of gratitude into your life is an exercise in subtlety and simplicity. It doesn't call for a standing ovation or a social media post; it's the silent pat on the back you give life for all the small things that go right. And over time, this habit of hushed thankfulness builds a resilience that buffers against the cacophony of daily hassles. So, take a moment, look around, and tip your hat to the minutiae. After all, they're the quiet constants in the ever-changing equation of life.

1. **The Morning Thank-You Note:** Starting your day with a mental thank-you note is akin to setting the tone of your personal soundtrack to one of appreciation. Before the world awakens your responsibilities and to-do lists, take a tranquil moment to acknowledge the small cogs in the machinery of your daily life. It could be the steadfast warmth of your bed that cradled you through the night or the faithful alarm clock that, albeit begrudgingly, wakes you up for a new day. These silent 'thank yous' whispered into the dawn light are like secret hand-shakes with the universe, acknowledging the comfort and constancy it provides.

This practice doesn't call for grand revelations or life-changing events to be grateful for. Peace can be found in the first light of morning, the familiar texture of a toothbrush, or the aroma of breakfast as it fills the space around you. It's a private ritual between you and the simplicity of living, a personal note of thanks to the universe for the unspoken promise of another day. As the day unfolds, this initial act of recognition keeps you anchored, reminding you that joy often resides in quiet corners.

And this isn't just about self-satisfaction; it's a ripple effect. The gratitude you cultivate within the quietude of morning radiates outward, influencing your interactions and perceptions throughout the day. It's an invisible thread that weaves through your daily tapestry, subtly yet significantly coloring your world with a hue of contentment. So, as the sun peeks through your curtains, let your first thoughts be brushed with gratitude, and watch how it subtly but surely brightens the canvas of your day.

2. **The Good Old Gratitude List:** In the whirlwind of daily life, a gratitude list stands as a steadfast reminder of the good that often goes unnoticed. It's the act of pausing amidst the chaos to note down the silver linings, the lifelines, the sparkles in the mundane. Whether it's a brief moment of solace in a busy day or the satisfaction of a well-made meal, these notes are your personal ledger of life's little blessings. Scribble them anywhere—a napkin, the back of a receipt, or a digital note on your phone—it's the act of recording that counts, not the medium.

The list need not be long or profound; sometimes, it's the simplicity that strikes the deepest chord. "Coffee was strong," "The cat curled up next to me," "Caught the green light all the way to work"—each entry is an affirmation of the pockets of peace and pleasure that dot your landscape. This tangible track record of positivity serves as a counterbalance to the often overwhelming ledger of life's deficits and demands. It's a concrete chronicle of the affirmative, a tangible tally that can be revisited in moments of doubt or gloom.

And while the list is a personal endeavor, its effects are far-reaching. Sharing your gratitude list can inspire others to notice their own daily gifts, creating a collective consciousness of appreciation. It's about transforming the routine into the remarkable and the pedestrian into the poignant. So, let each item on your list be a stepping stone towards a more mindful and thankful existence, building a bridge over the tumultuous waters of negativity and leading you to the serene shores of gratitude.

3. **The Positive Ping:** In a digital world often criticized for its coldness, the positive ping is a beacon of warmth. It's a digital hug, a virtual high-five, an emoji-laden expression of thanks. Taking a brief pause in your scroll to send appreciation into the ether can be a powerful connector. Not only does it make the recipient's day a little lighter, but it also reinforces your own focus on the positive aspects of your life. It's a modern-day version of tossing a penny into a wishing well, sending good vibes into the digital universe with the hope that they multiply.

This quick act of gratitude can bridge distances, mend fences, and bring smiles. It doesn't have to be elaborate; the beauty lies in its brevity and sincerity. "Thanks for the laugh," "Appreciated your advice today," or even a simple "Thinking of you" can carry immense weight in the digital realm. It's a reminder that behind every screen, there's a human heart that thrives on connection and acknowledgment.

Moreover, the positive ping is reciprocal; it boomerangs back to you in ways you might not expect. It fosters a cycle of kindness and recognition that spirals outward, creating a virtual environment rich with positive reinforcement. It transforms your inbox from a place of demands to a gallery of gratitude, and it reminds you that, even in the digital world, humanity and warmth can prevail. So, go ahead and hit send on that message of thanks—be an architect of affirmation in a landscape often starved for genuine connection.

4. The Dinner Debrief: In the evening, as you settle down for dinner, allow yourself a moment of reflection. It's a time to sift through the day's events and extract a kernel of positivity to savor alongside your meal. Perhaps it's the driver who let you merge into busy traffic or the unexpected compliment that brightened your afternoon. These moments, when shared over a meal, become more than just conversation; they're threads woven into the fabric of your relationships, strengthening the bond with your loved ones.

This ritual of sharing turns the dinner table into an altar of appreciation. It's a place where the day's triumphs, no matter how small, are given their due. It's an invitation to others to join in the celebration of the commonplace turned commendable. The practice of recounting these instances aloud can solidify them in your memory, transforming fleeting feelings of thankfulness into lasting impressions on your heart.

Engaging in this practice daily turns gratitude into a communal feast, where each person brings a dish of delights to the table. It's a shared experience that not only enriches the meal but enriches the soul. Over time, this habit will foster an environment where looking for the good becomes second nature, and expressing it becomes a joyous ritual. So, as you break bread, remember to also break open the repository of the day's gratitudes, and let them nourish you just as much as the food on your plate.

5. The Nightcap of Niceties: As the day draws to a close and you prepare to surrender to the comfort of your bed, indulge in a nightcap of niceties. Reflect on an interaction that added a sparkle to your day, savoring it as you would a fine wine. It's the cozy blanket of contentment that you wrap around yourself, a personal acknowledgment of the day's subtle yet significant high points. This could be as simple as the barista remembering your order or the way the sunset painted the sky on your commute home.

This final act of gratitude is a gentle but potent way to bookend your day. It sets a restorative tone for your slumber, ensuring that you drift off with thoughts tinted by the positivity of the day's interactions. It's a quiet affirmation that, despite any challenges, there were moments of genuine connection and kindness worth cherishing. It's a reminder that, in the grand narrative of your life, these are the scenes that matter, the ones that deserve a spotlight in the theater of your mind.

Incorporating this nightcap ritual into your routine is like planting a garden of good thoughts before bedtime, ensuring that your dreams are fertilized with the seeds of positivity. It doesn't require a grand gesture or lengthy process; it's as simple as a quiet thank you to the universe for its small gifts. And as you succumb to sleep, you do so with the knowledge that you've wrapped up the day in a shawl of thankfulness, ready to unwrap a new day of opportunities and blessings come morning.

Cultivating Joyful Moments: Cultivating joyful moments in the midst of our bustling lives can be akin to discovering a hidden playground in an urban jungle. It's about seizing those spur-of-the-moment opportunities for delight amidst our tightly packed schedules. I realized this during a particularly hectic week, when my to-do list was longer than a roll of toilet paper and just as daunting. Amidst this chaos, I found joy in the simplest of things: a perfectly brewed cup of coffee, a random smile from a stranger, or even the way the sunlight played through the leaves. It wasn't about carving out huge chunks of time for elaborate joy-inducing activities; it was about finding joy in the cracks of my everyday life.

I started by making small adjustments to my routine, turning mundane tasks into opportunities for joy. Cooking dinner wasn't just about feeding my family; it became an impromptu dance party with my favorite tunes blaring in the background. Morning commutes transformed from a time of stress to a period of learning and entertainment, where I'd listen to hilarious podcasts or audiobooks. These changes didn't require extra time or resources; they just needed a shift in perspective. By infusing these everyday moments with a sense of playfulness and appreciation, I began to experience a deeper sense of contentment and happiness.

The beauty of cultivating joy in this way is that it's contagious. My newfound approach to life started affecting those around me. Family dinners became more about sharing laughs than just eating, and even my colleagues noticed a change in my demeanor at work. We started sharing jokes and taking short breaks to simply enjoy each other's company. I learned that joy doesn't need an invitation; it just needs a little space to blossom. And once it takes root, it grows and spreads, turning even the most ordinary days into an adventure. So, as you navigate your busy life, remember that joy is waiting around every corner, ready to turn your daily script into a vibrant, laughter-filled narrative.

The Laughter Alarm:

The Laughter Alarm isn't just about disrupting your routine with a chuckle; it's a radical act of injecting playfulness into your day. When I first tried it, I was skeptical. But as the alarm rang and I shared a ridiculous dad joke with my colleague, the shift in energy was palpable. It was like a gust of fresh air into the stale room of daily tasks. From then on, the Laughter Alarm became my secret weapon against the midday slump, a reminder that joy doesn't need an appointment.

Implementing this practice is easy yet transformative. You can set multiple alarms throughout the day, each a prompt to pause and embrace a moment of lightness. It might feel awkward at first, like doing a solo dance in a crowd, but soon it becomes second nature. I found myself eagerly anticipating the next alarm, curious about how I could inject humor into that moment. It turned into a creative challenge, one that brought unexpected moments of connection with those around me.

The ripple effect of this practice is surprising. Your laughter can extend beyond personal joy, touching the lives of others around you. I noticed colleagues starting their laughter alarms, and the office buzzed with a newfound vibrancy. It's a testament to how a small act can create waves of positivity, turning a regular day into a series of joyful interludes.

The Humor Hunt:

The Humor Hunt is like a treasure hunt for your soul, where the prize is moments of pure, unscripted happiness. At first, it might seem like you're forcing yourself to look for humor, but soon you realize that life is riddled with funny moments just waiting to be noticed. I started with a simple rule: find one thing every day that made me smile. It could be as trivial as a funny bumper sticker or a toddler's nonsensical babble.

This daily mission soon became an adventure. I began to see the world through a lens of humor. The more I looked, the more I found – the couple bickering comically over groceries, the dog chasing its tail with relentless optimism, or even my own misadventures, like mistaking shampoo for conditioner. It turned my everyday landscape into a canvas of comedy.

Capturing these moments became a ritual. Each photograph or note was a reminder of the day's hidden humor. On tough days, revisiting these snippets was like flipping through a personalized comic book, each page a reminder that joy and laughter are ever-present, waiting to be discovered.

The Giggle Fit Challenge:

The Giggle Fit Challenge is about rediscovering the uninhibited joy of laughter, a sound that often gets muted in the humdrum of adult life. I introduced this to my friends during a dinner that was dangerously close to turning into a group therapy session. We set a timer and began laughing, initially forced, but within seconds, it evolved into genuine, contagious laughter. It was a reminder of the healing power of laughter, a natural stress reliever.

Integrating this challenge into your life is easy. Use it as a tool when the atmosphere gets tense or the mood needs lifting. It's a reminder that laughter is a universal language, one that can turn strangers into friends and sadness into joy. It's about letting go of the need to be composed all the time and embracing the silliness that's inherent in all of us.

The beauty of the Giggle Fit Challenge lies in its simplicity and its profound impact. It doesn't just lighten the mood; it strengthens bonds. The shared laughter creates a shared experience, a memory that's both endearing and empowering. It's a testament to how joy can be summoned, embraced, and shared, even in the most unlikely moments.

The Joy Jar:

The Joy Jar is more than just a container; it's a reservoir of positivity. On days when the world feels a little too heavy, reaching into the jar feels like reaching into a bag of magic. Each note is a reminder of a moment that brought a smile to my face. It could be something as small as a kind stranger holding the door or a particularly vibrant sunset.

Building this jar is a journey in itself. It starts with the conscious decision to recognize and record moments of joy. Each note is a commitment to acknowledging the beauty in everyday life. As the jar fills, it becomes a visual representation of the abundance of positivity that surrounds us, often unnoticed.

But the true magic of the Joy Jar unfolds when you reach in to retrieve a memory. It's like time travel, transporting you back to moments you've cherished. It's a reminder that happiness isn't always grandiose; it often resides in the quiet corners of our daily lives.

The Random Acts of Silly:

The concept of embracing silliness goes beyond just injecting humor into our daily lives; it's a form of subtle rebellion against the monotony and pressures of adulthood. It's an acknowledgment that life, even at its most serious, can still hold moments of lightness and laughter. I remember the day I decided to start my meetings with a corny joke. Initially, I was met with surprised chuckles and raised eyebrows, but soon it became a much-anticipated ritual. These small acts of silliness became a reminder for both myself and others that letting our guard down and reveling in pure, unadulterated fun is not only acceptable but necessary. They serve as a permit for us to momentarily break free from the daily grind and welcome the absurdity and delight found in everyday moments.

This practice of silliness is more than just a personal amusement; it's a bridge to connect with others on a deeper, more genuine level. In a world where digital interactions often replace personal connections, a shared laugh or a silly gesture can break down walls and foster a sense of camaraderie and closeness. I discovered that my own silliness could be the spark that ignites a lighter, more playful atmosphere in others. Whether it was through wearing a brightly colored tie to a formal event or sending a silly GIF in response to a standard email, these acts of whimsy invited others to join in the fun. It created a ripple effect, transforming the energy around me and making room for more authentic and joyful interactions.

Ultimately, embracing silliness is a celebration of our individuality and a challenge to the status quo. It's a statement that joy and laughter are essential, even in adulthood. By infusing our lives with these random acts of silliness, we're not just brightening our days; we're also reminding ourselves of the importance of playfulness and spontaneity. It's a way of saying that in the grand tapestry of life, each thread of laughter and each stitch of joy contributes to a more colorful, vibrant picture. So, go ahead and embrace your inner goofball. It might just be the most liberating and connecting thing you do today.

Renewing Love Continuously:

Alright, let's get down to brass tacks. Keeping love fresh is like trying to make your grandma's recipe for the first time. You're not entirely sure what you're doing, but you're determined to make it work, even if it means setting off the smoke alarm a couple of times. So, armed with a sense of humor and a willingness to embrace the absurd, I dove headfirst into the art of renewing love, and here's what I found out.

First up, we ditched the same old dinner and movie routine for what I call 'Wild Card Date Nights.' It's like drawing a random card from a deck – you never know what you're going to get. We ended up at a karaoke night, belting out tunes so off-key that even the microphone was cringing. Then there was the time we tried to cook a fancy meal together and ended up with something resembling alien cuisine. It wasn't about culinary perfection; it was about laughing over our culinary misadventures.

Next, I started the 'Love Note Guerrilla Warfare.' This involved sneaking little notes of affection into the most unexpected places. A cheeky 'I love you' hidden in a cereal box, a flirty message tucked into a sock drawer. Each note was a mini-surprise, turning our daily grind into a playful scavenger hunt. It was like sprinkling a little rom-com magic into our everyday life, minus the dramatic airport chase scenes.

Then we became amateur detectives in our own love story. We'd ask each other the most bizarre questions. "If you were a superhero, what would your superpower be?" It sparked conversations that were more twisty and intriguing than a mystery novel. It was like peeling back the layers of an onion, except with fewer tears and more laughter. Each answer was a doorway into a new, unexplored part of each other's minds.

And for the pièce de résistance: 'Freaky Friday' – a day where we switched roles. I tackled their to-do list, they tackled mine. Breakfast was a series of near-disasters, and let's not even mention what happened when I tried to do the laundry. It was a day of hilarity and chaos, but it left us with a deeper appreciation for each other's daily battles and a belly full of laughs.

By the end of these escapades, our love felt like it had been through a refresh cycle – a bit disheveled, but brighter and more vibrant. It turns out, reigniting the spark doesn't require fireworks; sometimes, it just takes a willingness to step out of your comfort zone, embrace the goofy, and laugh at the burnt toast moments of life. So here's to the crazy experiments, the unexpected adventures, and keeping the disco ball of love spinning, even if we sometimes trip over our own feet while dancing under it.

1. The 'What's New, Pussycat?' Quiz: So, I started this little game called the 'What's New, Pussycat?' Quiz, and honestly, it's like having your own personal comedy show. Every day, I'd come up with the most off-the-wall questions I could think of. "If you were a superhero, what would your superpower be?" or "Which historical figure would you want to be stuck in an elevator with?" The point wasn't to get into a deep philosophical debate (although that happened once over a discussion about being a spatula). It was about injecting a bit of absurdity into the daily grind.

Let me paint the scene: there we were, sitting at our usual breakfast nook, both of us scrolling through our phones, the epitome of modern disconnectedness. I dropped a question about which cereal character would make the best roommate. The look of bewildered amusement on their face was priceless. Suddenly, our monotonous morning transformed into an animated discussion about the pros and cons of living with Tony the Tiger. It was ridiculous, sure, but it was also the most we'd laughed on a Tuesday morning.

This game became our thing. It didn't matter if you were single, dating, or long-married; everyone got a kick out of it. Friends started doing it, too. It was like throwing a pebble into a pond and watching the ripples of laughter spread. The questions could be anything – from the absurd to the slightly more thoughtful. "If you could invent a holiday, what would it celebrate?" These whimsical inquiries led to stories and insights that I'd never have heard otherwise.

But the real magic? It was in the way these silly questions revealed layers of personality and thought I hadn't seen before. Who knew that a question about being a kitchen gadget could lead to a heartfelt conversation about creativity and usefulness? Or that debating the best strategy for a zombie apocalypse could be a metaphor for how we tackle life's challenges? The 'What's New, Pussycat?' Quiz turned out to be more than just a bit of fun; it was a portal to understanding each other in new, delightful ways. So, go on, ask a ridiculous question today. You might just be surprised at the conversation it cooks up.

2. Operation Sneaky Snuggles: Welcome to 'Operation Sneaky Snuggles', the covert mission I launched to bring a little more warmth into everyday life. Picture this: you're knee-deep in laundry, or maybe you're just lounging on the couch, and out of nowhere, boom! You're hit with a surprise hug. It's like being ambushed by a teddy bear – unexpected but totally delightful. At first, these random acts of affection were met with a mix of surprise and confusion. "What's gotten into you?" was the usual reaction, but let me tell you, it quickly turned into a game of hug tag.

It wasn't just about the physical act of hugging; it was about breaking the monotony of daily routines. You know, turning a standard Tuesday into a feel-good movie scene. There I was, sneaking up behind my partner while they were cooking, wrapping my arms around them, and for a moment, we'd forget about the boiling pasta. It was our mini timeout from the world, a secret bubble where only laughter and love existed.

And hey, singles, don't think this doesn't apply to you. Surprise your friends, your family, or even your pet with an unexpected squeeze. The beauty of Operation Sneaky Snuggles is its universal appeal. Everyone can use a hug, right? It's about creating a moment of connection in a world that often feels too busy to breathe. It turns the grocery aisle into a giggle fest or a walk to the car into a moment of togetherness.

But the real win? It's the ripple effect. These spontaneous snuggles started to change the vibe of our entire day. It was like each hug zapped away a bit of stress or worry. Our friends started to catch on, and before we knew it, we had a whole circle of sneaky snugglers. It's funny how something as simple as a hug can transform your day, turn strangers into friends, and remind you that in the hustle of life, there's always time for a little love and a lot of laughter. So go on, launch your own Operation Sneaky Snuggles – the world could definitely use more of it.

3. The Bizarre Date Night Challenge: Alright, strap in for the Bizarre Date Night Challenge, where we tossed the rulebook of romantic dinners and movies out the window. Our mission? To infuse some serious "What the heck?" into our date nights. Picture this: instead of the usual table for two, we're in the backyard, armed with flashlights, on a mission to find the hidden 'treasure' (spoiler: it was just a box of chocolates). But let me tell you, it was more thrilling than any fancy restaurant.

These dates were like jumping into a pool of quirky fun. Think making a fort out of blankets and pillows and binge-watching cartoons with popcorn battles, or having a goofy fashion show where we'd dress up in the most outrageous outfits we could find. The goal was to make each other laugh until our stomachs hurt. And guess what? It worked every time. It was about creating memories that could make us giggle on the gloomiest of days.

And hey, for all the single folks out there, you can totally rock this too. Call up some friends and organize a themed movie night or a cook-off where the weirdest dish wins. The idea is to turn an ordinary evening into a carousel of hilarity and bonding. The Bizarre Date Night Challenge is about embracing the spontaneous, the silly, and sometimes, the downright absurd.

So, go ahead, throw caution to the wind and your date night playbook out the door. Embrace the bizarre, the unexpected, the hilariously outlandish. Let's face it, life's too short for boring dates. So why not turn your love life (or social life) into a series of escapades that would leave even the most seasoned adventure-seeker in awe? After all, love - just like life - should be a story worth telling, and the best stories always have a twist of the unexpected.

4. The Blast from the Past Game: Let me take you on a trip down memory lane, where my partner and I turned reminiscing into an Olympic sport. Every week, we'd take turns sharing a favorite memory, creating our own personal "This is Your Life" show. "Hey, remember the time we thought it was a great idea to go camping without checking the weather?", I'd start, and off we'd go, reliving the adventure of getting soaked in the rain but ending up laughing under a makeshift tarp. These shared memories were like our own comedy and romance series, reruns that never got old.

These trips down memory lane were like opening a box of old photographs, each memory a snapshot of our time together. Sometimes it was a small moment, like that time we accidentally swapped lunches, leading to hilarious confusion and a newfound appreciation for each other's culinary dislikes. Other times, it was bigger stuff, like reminiscing about our first trip together, navigating a foreign city with just a map and a pocketful of excitement. It was a way to celebrate our history, to remember the steps that led us to where we are now.

And hey, singles, you're not left out of this game. Take a moment each week to remember a happy memory with friends or family. Reflect on the epic road trips with your closest friends or recall the times you've tried to bake a birthday cake, only to end up covered in frosting. These are the cherished moments that shape your journey, your friendships, and your life's narrative.

In the end, The Blast from the Past Game is more than just a trip down memory lane; it's a reminder of the resilience, laughter, and love that we've shared. It's a practice of weaving these memories into the fabric of our everyday life, ensuring that the past isn't just a shadow but a part of our present tapestry. So, whether it's with a partner or friends, let's keep those memories alive and kicking, because sometimes, looking back is the best way to appreciate where we stand today.

5. The 'Let's Get Learning' Experiment: In the grand experiment of love, my partner and I became eager students, signing up for the university of "Us 101." Picture this: two adults, often clueless but always game, diving headfirst into the deep end of new experiences. We started with something simple yet challenging – learning to cook a dish from a cuisine we'd never tried. There we were, aprons on, spices in hand, turning the kitchen into a laboratory of love and laughter (and a bit of culinary chaos).

Each new endeavor was like a puzzle piece, adding another layer to our understanding of each other. We tried our hands at pottery, our creations more reminiscent of abstract art than functional dinnerware. But it wasn't about the end product; it was the process – hands covered in clay, sharing stories, and discovering new quirks about each other. For singles, this is your cue to dive into a new hobby or interest. Ever fancied learning the guitar or understanding astrophysics? Go for it! Enrich your life with new layers of knowledge and fun.

These learning adventures became our weekly date with discovery. We signed up for dance classes, stepping on each other's toes more often than not, but always ending up in a fit of giggles. It was about moving out of our comfort zones and into a rhythm of shared growth. Singles, pair up with a friend for a dance class or tackle a challenging hike. Creating stories, learn new things, and add chapters to your book of life.

In essence, the 'Let's Get Learning' Experiment was our way of saying, "Let's not just grow old together; let's grow together." For couples, exploring new avenues of connection enriches the relationship; for singles, expanding horizons and celebrating self-growth add new dimensions to life's journey.

So, whether it's salsa dancing or speaking Spanish, let's turn life into a classroom where love is the favorite subject, and every lesson is a step towards a more fulfilled, joyful self.

As we wove these practices into the fabric of our love life, it was like injecting a rainbow into a sky that was already pretty blue. It wasn't just about adding color; it was about enriching the spectrum of our relationship. These daily quirks and adventures turned routine into romance and the mundane into magic. From the 'What's New, Pussycat?' quizzes over breakfast to the unexpected cuddle ambushes, each day was infused with a sense of playfulness and discovery.

Every bizarre date night, every shared giggle, and every new lesson learned together became a chapter in our ever-growing love story. It was like crafting a novel where each page crackled with the electricity of shared joy and mutual curiosity. For singles, these practices transformed the relationship with self, turning solitude into a celebration of independence and self-discovery. Whether it was laughing at a silly joke alone or dancing in the living room with no audience, the essence was the same: embracing life's little joys and finding happiness within.

What began as an experiment in keeping love fresh morphed into a lifestyle, a way of being that permeated every aspect of our relationship. It made us realize that love, much like life, thrives on renewal and rejuvenation. It's a garden that needs constant tending, a painting that evolves with each stroke, a story that unfolds with every word. And for those flying solo, it's a journey of self-love that radiates outward, attracting positivity and joy.

In conclusion, chapter 7 of our journey – "Celebrating Love Every Day" – stands as a tribute to nurturing love, whether shared with a partner or cultivated within oneself. This chapter recognizes that love's true essence cannot be quantified; it is found in the boundless, the intangible, and the eternal. As we turn the page to the next chapter of our lives, let's carry with us the laughter, the learning, and the love that makes every day a celebration. And remember, in the grand equation of life, love – in all its forms – is the constant that makes everything else add up.

Conclusion

♥

"The practice of love offers no place of arrival; it is a journey that is perpetually unfolding."

So, we were decluttering masters of our emotional closets, tossing out those outdated grudges and worn-out worries like last season's fashion faux pas. And finally, celebrating love every day – that's where we transformed everyday moments into episodes of our personal love sitcom, complete with laughter tracks and spontaneous applause.

Now, as we stand here at the conclusion, it's essential to remember that this journey doesn't have a final destination. Like the best kind of road trip, you try and grasp the scenery along the way, the pit stops, the unexpected detours, and yes, even the occasional flat tire. The '7 Simple Steps' are your GPS, guiding you through the highways and byways of love and life.

1. **Cultivating Self-Awareness:** We kicked off our journey with the fundamental step of self-awareness, which is about turning the spotlight inward and getting to know the real you - quirks, qualities, and all. This step is like peeling an onion; it might bring a tear to your eye, but it's crucial for

uncovering the core of who you are. The impact? A clearer understanding of your emotions, desires, and, most importantly, your boundaries. It's the first brick in the foundation of a fulfilled life and meaningful relationships.

2. **Healing From Within:** Next, we tackled the art of healing, patching up those emotional potholes that have jostled your journey. Healing isn't about erasing the past but rather drawing lessons from it and stepping forward with a heart unburdened. This step empowers you to let go of baggage that's been weighing you down, making space for new, healthier experiences and relationships.

3. **Communicating Authentically:** Here, we learned that true communication is the bridge between your heart and the world. Authenticity in your words and actions fosters deeper connections and trust. This step transforms your interactions, making them more meaningful. It's about being honest and open, turning conversations into pathways for genuine connection.

4. **Fostering Intimacy and Trust:** Building trust and deepening intimacy are about creating a secure, nurturing space for love to flourish. This step showed the importance of mutual respect, understanding, and the little acts that knit hearts closer. It's the daily maintenance of love, keeping the gears of your relationships well-oiled and smooth-running.

5. **Embracing Shared Growth:** Growth is not a solo journey. In this step, we explored how sharing dreams and supporting each other's personal goals can lead to a stronger bond. It's

like being each other's cheerleader and coach, celebrating victories and navigating challenges together. This step transforms relationships into dynamic partnerships where both individuals thrive.

6. **Letting Go of What No Longer Serves:** This step was about lightening the load by shedding old grudges and negative patterns. It's the emotional equivalent of decluttering, creating space for positivity and new experiences. The impact is profound as you unburden your heart and embrace the freedom that comes with forgiveness, taking steps forward on your path.

7. **Celebrating Love Every Day:** Finally, we capped it off with a daily celebration of love, finding joy in the small things, keeping the spark alive through gratitude, playful interactions, and continuous learning about each other. This step transforms everyday life into an ongoing love story, filled with moments of joy, laughter, and appreciation.

These seven steps, woven together, create a tapestry of a life lived with purpose, connection, and love. They're about transforming not just your relationships, but your entire approach to life, infusing each day with a sense of understanding, growth, and joy. As you continue to practice and revisit these steps, you'll find that they become less of a routine and more of a natural part of your life, leading to lasting inner peace and fulfilling relationships.

But here's the kicker – the journey doesn't end when you close this book. Nope, it's just the beginning. You're the driver in the seat of your love life, and these steps are your trusty co-pilot. Keep revisiting them, keep practicing, and keep reflecting. Whether you're cruising down the freeway or navigating a bumpy road, these steps will keep your emotional engine running smoothly.

The journey of love, like any great adventure, isn't about reaching a final destination. It's an ongoing exploration, a continuous cycle of learning, growing, and adapting. As you step out from the pages of this book and into the world, remember that each day offers a fresh opportunity to apply these steps. They're tools in your kit, ready to be used whether you're basking in the sunshine of joy or weathering a storm of challenges. The key is consistency. Just like watering a plant or tuning a guitar, these practices require regular attention to flourish. Keep them close, like a set of keys in your pocket, ready to unlock new levels of understanding and connection.

Think of these seven steps as your personal workout routine for the heart and mind. The more you practice, the stronger and more resilient your emotional and relational muscles become. Some days, it'll feel like a breeze; on others, it might feel like an uphill climb. That's okay. The beauty of this journey lies in its ups and downs. Each step, each repetition, adds depth and texture to your life's tapestry. And like any good workout, the benefits compound over time. You'll find yourself more equipped to handle the complexities of relationships, more adept at finding joy in the small things, and more at peace with yourself.

So, as we draw the curtains on this chapter, remember that your story continues to unfold with every step you take. Keep these lessons close to your heart. Reflect on them during quiet moments, discuss them with friends or partners, and most importantly, live them out in your daily life. Your journey towards a love-filled life is unique, and these steps are your compass, guiding you through the winding paths and open roads ahead. Embrace them, cherish them, and watch as they transform not just your relationships, but every aspect of your being. Here's to your journey, to your continuous growth, and to the endless celebration of love in all its forms. Keep turning the pages of your life with curiosity, courage, and a heart full of love.

As we say our goodbyes (for now), remember this: the love you've cultivated, the peace you've found, the relationships you've enriched – they're not just chapters in a book. They're chapters in your life, stories to be continued, pages to be filled. So go forth with your heart full and your eyes open. Embrace love in all its forms, and let it illuminate every corner of your life, from the break of dawn to the stars in the night sky.

There we have it, the end of our journey together in 'How To Be Loved'. But in truth, it's just another beginning. Here's to you, the hero of your story, stepping into a world where love is not just a word, but a way of life. Keep loving, keep learning, and above all, keep laughing – because, in the arithmetic of life, love + laughter = a life well-lived.

And so, as we close the pages of 'How To Be Loved,' we're not just ending a chapter but beginning a new one in the grand story of your life. This book may have been your guide, but the journey ahead is uniquely yours. You're stepping out equipped with tools, insights, and a heart richer in love. The love you've nurtured and the peace you've fostered are not confined to these pages; they're part of the fabric of your life, threads that will weave through every interaction, every challenge, and every joy.

Carry this love with you as you journey forward. Let it be the light that guides your way in the darkest of times and the joy that amplifies your brightest moments. Let it color your view of the world, turning the mundane into the magical and the ordinary into the extraordinary. Remember, the love you hold within has the power to touch not just your life but the lives of everyone around you. It's a force that can transform, heal, and uplift.

So here's to you, the reader, the dreamer, the lover. As you step out into the world, remember that every day is an opportunity to live out the lessons of love. Keep your heart open, your mind curious, and your spirit adventurous. And never forget that in the grand equation of life, love is the constant that makes everything add up. Here's to a life filled with love, laughter, and endless possibilities. Keep turning the pages of your life with love as your compass and joy as your path. You are the author of your story, and the best chapters are yet to be written.

www.ingramcontent.com/pod-product-compliance
Lightning Source LLC
Chambersburg PA
CBHW071424150726

48000CB00001B/465